Intervention in the Early Years

An evaluation of the High/Scope curriculum

Julie O'Flaherty

P.7
P.39, 42
P.49×50

© National Children's Bureau, 1995

ISBN 1 874579 58 X

Published by National Children's Bureau Enterprises, 8 Wakley Street, London EC1V 7QE. Telephone 0171 843 6000.

National Children's Bureau Enterprises is the trading company for the National Children's Bureau (Registered Charity number 258825).

Typeset by Books Unlimited (Nottm), NG19 7QZ.

Printed and bound in the United Kingdom by Biddles Ltd

Contents

List of Tables

The author

After graduating in Psychology from University College Dublin, Julie O'Flaherty undertook postgraduate work in both Applied Psychology and Statistics. Since 1993 she has been working in the field of early education. She is currently working in Dublin as a Research Officer for the IEA PrePrimary Project, an international study being conducted in 16 countries and coordinated by the High/Scope Educational Research Foundation, Michigan, USA. The study aims to examine early education provision, quality and its effects in participating countries.

Her published work includes *Evaluation of St Audeon's Parent Pre-School Health Promotion Project* and *Evaluation of a Childcare Training Course for Travellers*, a study undertaken on behalf of Barnardo's, Republic of Ireland and Horizon, as well as this book.

Foreword

Intervention in the Early Years is a professional and comprehensive evaluation of an early childhood intervention programme at Millbrook, Tallaght, a large 'new town' development on the outskirts of Dublin. Initiated by Barnardo's (Ireland), the core of the intervention was a High/Scope programme for children from families of marked socio-economic disadvantage. Although, as the evaluator points out, the small size of the sample and the composition of the contrast group make it difficult to ascribe the progress made by the children to the specific curriculum used, the evaluation clearly shows that the intervention was highly significant at local and national levels.

From its very foundation, the Irish education system has been confronted by a number of major – and still unresolved – problems. Relevant to the present study is the well-recorded degree to which educational outcomes in Ireland have been linked to socio-economic origins. Children of unskilled or unemployed parents living in segregated localities have had, comparatively, little chance of real success in primary school or of completing secondary education. In consequence, their entry into third-level education or employment is fraught with difficulty, as the Irish labour market is characterised by rising educational requirements and credentialism. Informed commentators argue that the children of the poor are, in reality, marginalised by school and leave it as soon as possible with an abiding sense of failure. In short, they are denied a fair start in life.

Is there a solution to this dysfunction of education systems, which, throughout the world, almost always proclaim equality of chances and yet manage to favour the children of the elite? To achieve some measure of equality, political will is essential to ensure that economic development serves all the children within a society. Increased attention must be given also to policies, structures and institutions which impinge directly on families, for example, to income and taxation issues, the quality of social and education services, housing and workplace conditions, local government and policing, urban planning. In most European Union countries, proactive measures are also taken vis-a-vis disadvantaged social groups. Compensatory programmes have been put into place, especially for pre-school and lower primary children, such as the *Zones d'enseignement prioritaires* in France or the *Opstapje* programmes in the Netherlands. Such programmes help young children acquire the social and cognitive skills required by formal schooling and give them a good start in the crucial first years in school. In France, Belgium and other countries, these programmes are normally centre-based. In Sweden, the Netherlands and in several Latin America countries, more emphasis is placed on supporting families to rear children and provide a learning environment in the home.

In Ireland too, the climate of the 1990s has been favourable to raising awareness about child poverty and education issues, for instance, significant progress was made through the signing into law of the Child Care Act in July 1991, the ratification of the Convention on the Rights of the Child in September 1992, the European Council's Recommendation on Child Care in March 1992, and through the manifest concern of successive governments to co-ordinate action for children, first through the Department of Health and at present, through a Minister for State with special responsibility for Child Care. The Department of Education has also been active in attempting to compensate for social or economic disadvantage suffered by children, through the *Home/School Liaison Project* and the *Early Start* pre-school initiative. The recent white paper on education *Charting Our Education Future* bodes well: it sets equality as one of the guiding principles of Irish education and promises to 'include strategies for the earliest feasible intervention to support children at risk of educational failure'. Statutory initiatives are matched by a growing, professional voluntary sector, as manifested by the Focus on Children summits in Dublin and Belfast in September 1994.

Yet much remains to be done. Among the European Union countries, Ireland ranks remarkably low in its investment in the care and education of its young. Provision for children aged 0-2 years is particularly weak, and although education services for children aged 3-5 are available, these older children find themselves generally in overcrowded classrooms, without the care and nutritional support which characterise the kindergartens or *maternelles* of the continental European countries. In addition, teaching staff, though of excellent quality, are rarely trained in the philosophy and methods of early childhood education, and their task in infant schools is made extremely difficult by unfavourable staff/pupil ratios. Sufficient awareness of the crucial impact on educational achievement that significant investment in pre-school and lower primary school can achieve is still not present.

The accumulated research on early childhood intervention, however, is clear: good early childhood programmes prepare children for school, influence their productivity and income levels later on in life and reduce public expenditure significantly by lowering health, welfare and education costs. Where school readiness is concerned, early intervention promotes timely school enrolment, improves social and cognitive skills and enables children to avoid the failure trap of the lower primary cycle. The beneficial effect of early development programmes is particularly pronounced for traditionally disadvantaged groups, such as rural children from isolated areas and urban children from low socio-economic backgrounds.

The social argument in favour of early intervention programmes is no less strong. In contemporary industrialised democracies in which the goal of equal employment opportunities for women is pursued, families with young children need not only income support but also accessible childcare and family services. In poor localities where single parenthood and marriage separations are a growing phenomenon, such services have become vital as a means of caring for the children, of building up competence in families and of bringing the residents of disaffected housing estates to a consciousness of community and the possibility of local action. What is at stake here is not just better income distribution or the provision of social services but of supporting people to participate, to take charge of their own lives.

The Millbrook Nursery programme in Tallaght is an excellent example of affirmative action in favour of deprived children and their families. To have broken the vicious circle leading from poverty to educational failure, albeit for a limited number of children, is no small achievement. After participation in the programme, the Millbrook children entered primary school successfully and made steady progress throughout the lower grades. Nor do the benefits of the programme stop at learning achievement. Apart from the feelings of contentment which the children experienced while at Millbrook, the battery of tests used by the evaluator demonstrates also the growth of personal competence, sociability and adaptive behaviour. As one mother expressed it:

'It's helped me a lot as well. For ages, I couldn't do anything with him. He would just follow me everywhere, couldn't do anything without me. Now I think he just trusts me, that I'm coming back when he's dropped in the morning. He's become so independent.'

Because it provides a positive testimony to the High/Scope approach to early childhood learning, the evaluation of the Millbrook project is not without interest at the international level. Although not as probative as the longitudinal research on the Perry Preschool Project, it demonstrates how far-sighted David Weikart and his team were in choosing to intervene at the pre-school level in order to break the cycle of disadvantage. Weikart's trust in the inner autonomy and learning motivation of children was remarkable, as was his insistence on the structure quality of the pre-school curriculum – adequate funding, favourable staff/pupil ratio, appropriate room arrangement and materials, team facilitation and evaluation, clear understanding of the respective roles of children and facilitators, shared core method and daily routine, focus on child learning through the key experiences, continuous monitoring, parent involvement.

Kagan and Zigler (1987) have warned however, that 'we cannot simply inoculate children in one year against the ravages of a life of deprivation.' The struggle against poverty and exclusion must take place at different levels of society. The knowledge, attitudes and practices of the people, and especially of parents, need attention; community action and local development structures need to be established; the training and institutional capacities of local government need to be reinforced and above all, national commitment to child and family policies needs to be present. If governments lack an adequate vision of society and the political will to invest in the potential of all the children, social division and exclusion will continue to exist, despite the efforts made at pre-school level. In short, though the benefits for the individual children reached by sporadic early intervention programmes may indeed be great, a more systemic approach is needed at the level of a nation. It is to be hoped that the Millbrook initiative will be studied closely by the many voluntary and statutory agents working toward this goal in Ireland and elsewhere.

John Bennett, Co-ordinator
Early Childhood and Family Education Programmes, UNESCO[1]

---

1   The views and opinions expressed in this Preface are those of the author and do not in any way commit UNESCO

Acknowledgements

The successful completion of any research project relies upon the support and efforts of others beyond the research team. This project is no exception; there are many people who we wish to thank for their help and co-operation.

Firstly, the project would never have happened without the support of staff at Barnardo's, both in Britain and in Ireland. Nora Dixon, then co-ordinator of research at Barnardo's UK, commissioned the research and saw it safely on its way. Continuing success depended on staff from Barnardo's in Dublin – everyone at the nursery, in particular Maria O'Reilly, Irene Milner and Patricia Murphy, were enormously welcoming and gave so generously of their time; we greatly appreciated the encouragement of managers – from those at the project to the Director. The willingness of Barnardo's to provide office space and administrative support to the researchers from the National Children's Bureau greatly eased any problems of long distance management. Many thanks to them for providing such a friendly and efficient base.

We also wish to express our thanks to those who participated in the research; the principals and teachers of the schools; playgroup leaders for information on Group B children; the parents of the children. Most important of all we thank the children and wish them all good fortune for the future.

We are very grateful for the expert assistance we received when undertaking the research and preparing this book; Eilis Hennessy offered support and advice to the researchers in Dublin and the Statistics Department at Trinity College Dublin provided assistance with the statistical analysis; Joan Sharpe and Serena Johnston from the High/Scope Institute UK kept us informed of new developments in High/Scope and Dorothy Rouse Selleck from the Early Childhood Unit at the National Children's Bureau offered most helpful and insightful comments throughout the project.

Thanks are due also to Noirin Hayes at the Early Childhood Research Centre in Dublin.

The early research on this project was undertaken by Catherine Daly. Unfortunately, due to ill health, Catherine left mid-way. Julie O'Flaherty was appointed as research officer, and had the very difficult task of coming into the project at this point. However Julie's determined approach to the research is evidenced by the publication of this book. My thanks to both Catherine and Julie for their hard work, and for the respect which they gave to all those participating in the research.

The Research Department at the Bureau is dependent on the support of many other Bureau colleagues, in particular the Library and Information Service, the Early Childhood Unit, and the Publications Department. Their assistance on this project was particularly appreciated given the external, indeed the international, location of the researchers.

On behalf of the Research Department of the National Children's Bureau grateful thanks for the support and help we have received from you all.

Ruth Sinclair
Director of Research
National Children's Bureau
April 1995

Introduction

Those who attended a high-quality, active learning pre-school program at ages 3 and 4 have half as many criminal arrests, higher earnings and property wealth, and greater commitment to marriage.

For every $1 invested in High/Scope it is estimated to have saved the tax payer $7 in terms of reduced expenditure on special education, criminal justice system costs and lost tax revenue. (Schweinhart and others, 1993.)

These quotations highlight key findings from a longitudinal study undertaken in the USA. This compares the outcomes for a group of children who attended a High/Scope day centre in the 1960s with a group that received no pre-school service. Such claims are obviously of great interest to those concerned with early childhood education – academics, trainers, practice developers, providers of services and, not least, policy-makers. How relevant is such an approach to young children on this side of the Atlantic? Indeed does High/Scope offer anything new or different from current early years curricula? What impact might the High/Scope curriculum have on disadvantaged children in the British Isles? These are the themes addressed by the research study reported in this book.

The High/Scope curriculum was introduced into the USA in the 1960s as part of the Head Start programme. This was a programme aimed at reducing the educational disadvantage of children from socially and economically deprived backgrounds. The impact of the High/Scope curriculum has been subject to rigorous research and evaluation over many years. The original study, known as the Perry Preschool Project, lasted from 1962 to 1967. Subsequent research and the continuing development of the curriculum has been undertaken at the High/Scope Educational Research Foundation at Ypsilanti, under the direction of David Weikart.

Although High/Scope has been in use in the USA for over 30

years, it was not until the mid-80s that the first training course was set up in Britain. Since then, there has been a gentle but steady expansion in the use of High/Scope.

As a major provider of day care services to disadvantaged children, the child care charity, Barnardo's, was seeking in the mid-80s to enhance the quality of its early years services, and began to rethink its curriculum development. Barnado's became sufficiently interested in the High/Scope approach to support the early training initiatives. In 1986 Barnardo's in the Republic of Ireland decided to appoint a full-time High/Scope Trainer to introduce the High/Scope curriculum into its Millbrook day nursery in Tallaght, a very deprived suburb of Dublin.

In 1991 Barnardo's asked the National Children's Bureau to undertake a research project which would evaluate the impact of the introduction of the High/Scope curriculum at Millbrook. This study had four aims. These were to provide:

- an insight into the operation of High/Scope at the Millbrook Nursery as perceived by the staff and parents;
- an indication of how well-prepared the nursery 'graduates' were for starting primary school;
- an overview of the children's progress in primary school, one and two years after leaving the nursery;
- an indication of how these children were functioning – cognitively, emotionally and socially – as compared to a peer group who had not graduated from Millbrook.

This book reports the findings from the study. The results from the research are set in a broad context which includes: the current knowledge-base on the impact of early childhood education; the structure of educational provision in Ireland; a profile of the research area; and a discussion of the impact of social and economic disadvantage on educational opportunity.

Chapter 1 starts by exploring the characteristics of different early years services and examines the findings from available research on the impact of such services. The structure and range of educational services in Ireland is described in Chapter 2, together with a review of the relationship between poverty and educational disadvantage – a crucial factor in an area such as Tallaght which experiences such depth of deprivation. Chapter 3 introduces and describes the main elements of the High/Scope curriculum, comparing and contrasting them with other well-established early years curricula. Details of the research project are presented in Chapter 4. This chapter sets out the aims of the project, the methods employed, and a description of the children who make up the two sample groups, including information about their backgrounds.

Chapter 5 paints a picture of what a High/Scope nursery looks like, and describes how the principles of the curriculum were translated into practice at the Millbrook Nursery. The main findings from the research are presented in Chapter 6. This chapter brings together assessments of the impact of High/Scope from a variety of perspectives and using a wide range of quantitative and qualitative data. The chapter also provides a comparison between the two groups – the High/Scope 'graduates' and the other preschool group – in terms of their social, emotional and cognitive development during their first two years of schooling. Finally, this chapter compares the research findings from this study against others, in particular those reported from the early Perry Preschool Project.

1. Early years education: researching its impact

The nature of early childhood education

With more and more mothers now in full-time employment, the traditional first real separation experienced by a mother and her child at the start of primary schooling has been replaced by a date which occurs much earlier in the life of the child. Child care for very young children may be necessary because of parental employment; for the child aged three or over the emphasis shifts to care plus education. Even where mothers are the full-time carers for their children, in a majority of cases some kind of introduction to education before formal schooling is desirable. Hence, as we prepare to enter the twenty-first century, the need for early childhood education is more important than ever before.

In the first section of this chapter we will examine the varieties of early childhood educational provision that exist, the numbers actually using such services and the aims of these services. Compensatory and mainstream pre-school education programmes in many parts of the world are also reviewed. The final section attempts to pinpoint the reasons why some education programmes are more effective than others.

Pre-school classification

What exactly do we mean by the term early childhood education? The pre-school environment can have a variety of forms – care in the home by parents, relatives or paid employees; day care in another home, for example by a childminder; nurseries or crèches for infants and older children; mixed-age centres; playgroups; kindergartens.

Sylva (1994b) defined the child's early learning as learning which occurs outside the home before school entry. She included in this category nursery schools and classes, day nurseries or child care centres, and playgroups but excluded home care and child-minders with the rationale that their aim is primarily care.

The National Children's Bureau has compiled a comprehensive list of pre-school services in Britain (National Children's Bureau, 1995); a briefing paper by the National Commission on Education similarly describes the range of pre-schools services in the UK (Sylva and Moss, 1992). The same types of services exist in Ireland, albeit in lesser numbers and without the same regulatory framework.

In summarising this diverse picture the National Children's Bureau first distinguishes between the providing sector: the independent/private/voluntary sector and the local authority/maintained/statutory sector. A further distinction is drawn between care services and education services, although it is noted that increasingly centres in both sectors offer various combinations of day care and education.

Private and *voluntary nurseries* include several types of group: community nurseries, all-day playgroups, workplace nurseries, partnership nurseries and private 'for profit' nurseries. All provide full or sessional care and are often fee-paying. *Local authority day nurseries* provide full- or part-time day care for children under five years, although few nurseries take children under 18 months. Most places are given to children whose families are experiencing health or social difficulties. Many centres are now working with parents and children together rather than simply providing day care; these are sometimes known as *family centres*. *Combined nursery centres* offer an integrated service to children from a few months to five years of age, combining day care and nursery education. Many also offer informal support such as parent and toddler groups or toy libraries. They are usually open from early morning until 5 or 6 pm, for most weeks of the year. Such centres are usually staffed by teachers and nursery nurses; some also employ social workers and health visitors.

Local authority nursery schools or classes provide free education for children between the ages of two and a half and five. Nursery classes are part of infant or primary schools; nursery schools are separate schools. Most children attend for either a morning or an afternoon session. *Private nursery schools* are fee-paying and are usually open for the length of the school day. An increasing number of primary schools admit children to *reception classes* before they are five, many attending full-time. Often staffing, equipment and curriculum are more appropriate to children aged five plus.

Childminders look after children under five (and also older children outside school hours) usually in the childminders own home. Childminding is usually a private arrangement between minder and parents and may be offered for all or part of the day, usually all year round. In some cases local authorities may sponsor children at childminders; this may be called community childminding or day foster care.

Other services available include those provided by *nannies, toy libraries, parent and toddler groups, play buses* and *crèches*. Nannies are employed privately by parents to look after children in the family home. Toy libraries lend selected toys and equipment to children and families. Originally established for parents of children with special needs, they are now more widely available and some have been established for childminders and playgroups. Some are run by parents; others by local authorities, health services, schools and voluntary groups (for example, Barnardo's runs several toy libraries in various parts of Dublin). Some may provide an informal setting in which health care and assessment can be carried out. Parent and toddler groups are small informal groups which offer play opportunities for children (usually under three) and companionship for their parents (who must accompany them). Play buses are special buses converted to accommodate toys and equipment for a small playgroup, or parent and toddler group – such as the two play buses operated by Barnardo's in Dublin for Irish Traveller children. Crèches provide informal short-term group care for children while their parents are engaged in other activities such as attending classes or shopping. However, more and more, services which cater for young children are encompassing both care and education.

Pre-school attendance

At least 71 million children below the age of six are enrolled in some form of pre-school programme, according to a UNESCO survey of 88 countries. In almost every country, this provision is for children between the ages of three and six. UNESCO estimated that in 1988 there was a global gross pre-primary enrolment rate of just under 30 per cent. This varied from an average of about 5 per cent in Sub-Saharan Africa to more than 67 per cent in Europe (UNESCO, World Education Report, 1991). An important consideration regarding access to pre-school environments is whether the particular form of pre-school care or education is privately or publicly funded. Privately-run pre-schools by their very nature exclude disadvantaged children, whereas publicly-run pre-school environments are open to all.

The aims of the early childhood education

Given the range and diversity of pre-school programmes, is it possible to establish the aims of these programmes? According to the National Association for the Education of Young Children (NAEYC), the rationale for day care and nursery school, in the short term, is to provide 'a safe and nurturing environment that promotes the physical, social, emotional and cognitive development of young children while responding to the needs of families' (Bredekamp, 1987, p.52). An investigation of the literature regarding early childhood education indicates that the pre-school services outlined at the beginning of this chapter set out to fulfil a range of purposes, for instance: to offer care and protection to children from deprived or neglectful home backgrounds; to provide a secure and stimulating environment in which young children can socialise with each other in a group (and which can also be seen as a preparation for school); to encourage cognitive and language development; to provide support to parents, especially lone parents, in caring for their children. Implicit in some of these services is the additional aim of trying to redress social inequality by providing extra help to children from poor, disadvantaged backgrounds, in the belief that this will enable them to enter formal schooling on a more equal footing with their peers.

In the long term the hope is that pre-school education provides a solid educational and social basis upon which the child can build and develop for the rest of his or her life.

> In today's ever-changing, fast-paced and increasingly interdependent society, we must educate our children to think, to discern value, to read for meaning, and above all, to function independently with an intact sense of self esteem. We don't know exactly what job skills will be required in the next century but we do know these are qualities which will be needed in those who succeed. (Griffin, 1990, cited in Power (1993))

While it is very appropriate to look for long-term outcomes from early years provision, we must recognise that what really matters is the actual pre-school experience for the child at the time. If the child is mixing with peers, is being cognitively stimulated and, most of all, is enjoying the experience, while the parent is secure in the knowledge that his or her child is getting good-quality care or education, this may be thought to be a sufficient aim. If in addition, this has long-term benefits to the child, so much the better.

In sum, defining 'pre-school provision' is no straightforward task. Early childhood services can mean different things to different people, take a variety of forms, even differing with respect to their aims.

Researching early childhood programmes

It is not surprising that there has been much interest in evaluating the effects of pre-school with respect to both short and longer-term outcomes. Research concerning the effects upon children's development has been carried out worldwide, but without doubt the USA has been the 'front runner' in terms of evaluative studies. However, it must be recognised that it is not always easy to compare pre-school provision and its effects across countries:

> ...consideration of research from within one country will present a distorted picture because the political and cultural limitations of any one country will restrict the range of pre-school environments offered to children, thus limiting the evidence for consideration. A comprehensive understanding of issues requires the integration of research across national boundaries, and a collaborative approach by researchers. (Melhuish, 1993, p.21.)

There are two major factors that differentiate pre-school environments: the degree to which they have care or education as their primary function, and the age of the child.

Early childhood programmes may be formal and explicitly educational, hence providing an early education for the child. On the other hand, they may provide day care for the very young child without a specific emphasis on education. However, the distinction between these two categories is becoming increasingly blurred as the importance of integrating these two concepts is more recognised: 'Quality care is educational and quality education is caring.' (Drummond, Rouse and Pugh, 1992.) As Burchinal, Lee and Ramey (1989) conclude, high-quality day care appears to affect cognitive growth positively in socio-economically disadvantaged children, and may even aid in preventing the patterns of intellectual underachievement that are too often observed in children from poor backgrounds. Similar objectives were implicit in the pre-school service offered by Millbrook Nursery.

The second distinction is by age. In very broad terms, day care most often refers to services for children under three years, whereas education is concerned with children over three years. Participants in the Millbrook Nursery study were aged three years and over.

In the following section we will examine some of the research evidence regarding the programmes that are aimed at providing an early education for children between the ages of three and five or six years. These programmes are distinguished according to the type of child that the service targets – and referred to as mainstream and compensatory. We have designated mainstream pre-school as open access, the kind of general pre-school service which is available to all children. Compensatory pre-schooling is more specific in its orientation. It is aimed at those children who are from socially and economically disadvantaged backgrounds and hence may be deemed to be at risk of educational underachievement. In this respect, pre-school aims to compensate for possible deficits at home, such that children will be on a par with their more advantaged peers when they start school.

Mainstream pre-school education

In recent years, in both the UK and further afield, a number of studies evaluating mainstream education have been carried out. Many of these have indicated the advantages that providing good quality pre-school education can have, and some have even attempted to pinpoint the forms of pre-school education which are superior.

McCartney and others (1982) investigated environmental differences among day care centres in Bermuda and their effects on children's language, social and emotional development. (Only children aged three years and older who attended a target centre for six months or more were included in the study.) They found that higher-quality day care environments appeared to have important positive effects on children's language, social and emotional development.

Jowett and Sylva (1986) compared the effects of well-resourced local authority nursery education with poorly resourced playgroups managed by parents working on tight budgets. They found that the nursery education 'graduates' demonstrated higher motivation for school, were more persevering when they encountered obstacles in their work and more learning-oriented when they approached the teacher. Furthermore, the study demonstrated that the kind of pre-school education a child experiences affects the ease with which she or he begins school.

Osborn and Milbank (1987) conducted a study which was based on data obtained in the Child Health and Education Study (CHES), a national longitudinal survey of all children born in one week of 1970. They followed up a sub-sample of 9,000 children at the ages of five and ten, looking at ability, attainment and behaviour. Their overall findings provided conclusive evidence that pre-school education provided by ordinary nursery schools and playgroups can have a positive effect on the cognitive development of the children who attend them. Furthermore, they found that the regime in normal infant reception classes may be less appropriate for the under-fives. They ranked the kinds of pre-school experiences which were associated with the best outcomes in terms of the effects on the children, and found playgroups to be superior to day nurseries. However, the fact that the children from most disadvantaged homes were the children attending day nurseries, and the children attending the playgroups were primarily more middle-class, meant that their finding of superiority of one kind of provision over another was not reliable.

These studies indicate that the quality of the pre-schooling that children receive is a significant factor in terms of how well they fare. This issue of quality is a very important one and will be explored in greater detail later in this chapter (page 18).

Shorrocks and others (1992) carried out a national evaluation of the first year of the full SATs (Standard Assessment Tests) in 1991, and a follow-up study in 1992, using a large sample of children. These SATs are obligatory in all maintained schools for all seven-year-olds in England and Wales. In the 1991 sample, about half the children had had pre-school experience of some kind, either at playgroup, nursery class or nursery school. When compared with children who had had no such experience, there were significant differences in their favour for both English and Mathematics, but not for Science. More detailed analyses indicated that children with pre-school experience scored significantly higher in reading and writing. In 1992 similar samples and procedures were used. At the total subject levels (English, Mathematics and Science) there were differences in favour of those with nursery school or class experience in all three subjects, which reached statistical significance in English and (unlike 1991) in Science (Shorrocks and others, 1993).

Compensatory pre-school education

Pre-school programmes worldwide

Examination of the research now available indicates that there are long-term benefits to be derived from well-planned pre-school provision. Furthermore, if children in mainstream education are seen to benefit from pre-schooling, it seems logical to assume that disadvantaged children have even more to gain. In fact, several studies suggest that while the impact of early education is found in all social groups it is strongest in children from disadvantaged backgrounds. In this section no causal link between pre-school education and, for example, academic success is assumed; instead research findings which indicate that good-quality pre-school education enhances the life chances of disadvantaged children are highlighted.

In 1969, an 'enrichment' pre-school with a structured programme was commenced as part of the 'Arid Zone Project' in the town of Bourke, New South Wales, Australia. The programme, aimed at an almost equal mix of aboriginal and white children, was based principally upon the direct-instruction design developed by Bereiter and Engelmann (1966), though it was modified to include Australian content and recently developed instructional techniques. The rationale underlying this design was that the teacher initiates activities and the child responds to them. On evaluating the effects of the pre-school programme upon the children, results indicated marked gains in most of the measures (for example, cognitive) although such gains were subsequently eroded, comparable to what was being reported in the USA. Those children who could be located were tested ten years after they first attended the pre-school and results showed that they registered average IQ scores, whereas before the pre-school experience these scores were, overall, below average. According to de Lacey and Ronan (1986) it seems likely that the pre-school experience was the major contributor to these results. On the basis of this, they concluded that pre-school would provide the opportunity to members of disadvantaged cultures (aboriginals in this case) to learn the valued skills and behaviours necessary for participation in mainstream society.

A study of child development in Malaysia found that pre-school programmes helped disadvantaged children to gain cognitive, language and socio-emotional skills (Chiam, 1991). Programmes in Colombia, Brazil, Haiti, India and Thailand have produced similar results (Haddad and others, 1990).

Longitudinal follow-up of children who attended the Rutland Street Project, a compensatory pre-school project in Dublin, Ireland (Kellaghan and Greaney, 1992), found that participants were more likely to take public examinations and to complete second level education than children who had no such pre-school experience. However follow-up of a group of children in a similar pre-school programme in Dublin as compared to a group of children who had had no pre-school experience failed to find any significant differences with regard to intellectual functioning, social/emotional behaviour and reading ability as the children progressed through primary school. However, some significant differences were apparent at an early stage with regard to reading levels and social/emotional behaviour in favour of the pre-school group (O'Flaherty, and others, 1994).

Pre-school programmes in the USA

Without doubt most interest in the concept of compensatory education has originated from the USA. In the 1930s and '40s, the question of the heritability and alterability of intelligence prompted much research. Skeels demonstrated the cumulative effects of inadequate home environments on the intelligence of children (Skeels and Fillmore, 1937), and the positive effects of altering such environments during the pre-school years (Skeels and others, 1938). His studies were heavily criticised, and he was not vindicated until the 1965 publication of his monograph detailing the adult status of his 125 original subjects (Skeels, 1965). Data reported in this monograph supported his position that nurture was as important as nature in human development and, along with a landmark book by Hunt (1961), justified the potential importance of early intervention (Casto and White, 1993). Since then hundreds of research studies have been conducted to investigate the efficacy of early intervention programmes for children with disabilities, 'disadvantaged' children and children 'at risk'. Unfortunately, much of this research, particularly that with children who have disabilities, suffers from serious methodological flaws, narrow definition of outcomes, and/or inadequately implemented interventions (Dunst and Rheingrover, 1981; Farran, 1990; Simeonsson, Cooper and Scheiner, 1982).

During the 1960s the public education system in the USA was handling its 'problem learners' chiefly in one of three ways: (1) referral to outside agencies to adjust the child for better behaviour and achievement; (2) referral to the special services staff of the school to counsel the child and family or to 'hold' the youngster in a special education class; (3) retention of the child in grade by 'failing' him or her in an effort to help the child learn the skills and behaviours appropriate to one grade level before advancing to the next. Each of these methods had severe shortcomings, particularly the remedy of requiring students to repeat grades until they learned the necessary skills. In Ypsilanti, for example, this practice produced the outlandish result of approximately 505 of all ninth-graders being from one to five years behind in grade, and a 50 per cent dropout rate, with legal school-leaving occurring as early as seventh grade. Moreover, this problem was not significantly different from that of any other middle- or working-class community in the USA.

These circumstances provided some of the impetus for the launch of the Ypsilanti Perry Preschool Project in 1962 (the most directly relevant longitudinal study to the present research) and the launch of National Headstart in 1965. National Headstart aimed to prepare disadvantaged children from all over the USA for entrance to kindergarten so that they would be on a par with their middle-class peers. Evaluation of these projects has been ongoing. The Consortium for Longitudinal Studies – a large-scale collaborative exercise – pooled together the results from studies of 11 pre-school programmes under the Headstart Initiative including those of the Perry Project (Lazar and others, 1982). These results indicated that attendance at excellent, cognitively oriented pre-school programmes was associated with later school competence. Pre-school 'graduates' were less likely to be assigned to 'special' education or to be held back in grade while their peers moved up, and (where data were available) were more likely to be in employment. Interviewers found that pre-school 'graduates' were more likely than the control group to give achievement-related answers to the invitation: 'Tell me something you've done that made you feel proud of yourself.' When parents were questioned about attitudes towards school performance, mothers of pre-school 'graduates' expressed more satisfaction with their children (even after controlling for the actual performance of each child). When asked what kind of job they would like for their child in the future, mothers replied skilled or managerial jobs. Taken together with the 'harder' outcomes, the attitudinal findings suggested that early education changed the achievement orientation of the family. Mothers whose children attended pre-school expected more from their children, and these expectations were fulfilled (Sylva, 1994a).

Each of these pre-school programmes was well-planned and high-quality (a concept which we will examine in more detail later), and each had been designed as a research project from the outset. The aim of the research component was to examine any immediate or longer-term differences in the performance of children who received the programme compared to control groups of equally disadvantaged children who did not. The scientific merit of this consortium study has been thoroughly tested and found to be rigorous, reliable and valid, and does not suffer from the flaws identified earlier by Dunst and Rheingrover; Farran; Simeonsson and colleagues: 'Lazar's work is distinguished by meticulous care in collecting and analysing the interviews and records.' (Sylva and David, 1990.)

In Chicago, in the mid-60s, an experimental programme was set up to provide long-term (four to six years) experience of early childhood education beginning at age three (Fuerst and Fuerst, 1993). An evaluative study published in 1976 (Fuerst, 1976) found that children who had completed the programme scored considerably higher than their peers in similar neighbourhoods as well as nationally and locally. In the mid-80s, a 15-year longitudinal study was undertaken by the Department of Research and Evaluation of the Chicago Board of Education for some 3,000 children in the public school system who had been exposed to a less extended one, or two-year pre-school education in 1973–4, along with 1,700 children not receiving such education (Rice, 1989). Results were, however, less conclusive, indicating that the reading and maths scores of children with pre-school education still did not show any advantages over those without pre-school education. Similarly, the graduation rates of youngsters with one or two years of pre-school education were no better than those children without it. However, in 1984 Fuerst and Fuerst began a comparative study of 683 children who were exposed to the six original programmes for four or more years. They were compared to a similar number of controls (who came from the same neighbourhood and were of the same age) who did not take part in early childhood programmes. Their findings corroborated the findings of the earlier 1976 study, indicating that when tested in the second grade most of the children in this study who had experienced four to five years of pre-primary and primary school education achieved reading and maths scores 'virtually on a par, if not higher, than the average of children in the same grade in the general community and the nation'.

Cryan and others (1992) reported a definite link between pre-school attendance and subsequent success at school. The relationship between pre-school attendance and cognitive test performance was evident even at the end of second grade. Furthermore, kindergartners with prior pre-school experience were rated more positively by their teachers on a behavioural measure than were pupils with no such experience. A study by Lee and others (1990) suggested positive effects from pre-school rather than of Headstart per se.

The Perry Preschool Project

Probably the most conclusive of the 11 Consortium studies, and hence the best-known, was the Perry study (using the High/Scope curriculum) which examined the lives of 123 African Americans born in poverty and at high risk of failing in school (Schweinhart and others, 1993). At ages three and four, these individuals were randomly divided into a programme group who received a high-quality, active learning pre-school programme and a no-programme group who received no pre-school programme. At 27 years old, 95 per cent of the original study participants were interviewed, with additional data gathered from their school, social services and arrest records. The two groups were compared in several dimensions. The findings were statistically significant, as detailed below:

- Social responsibility: by age 27, only one-fifth as many programme group members as no-programme group members had been arrested five or more times (7% vs 35%), and only one third as many had been arrested for drug dealing (7% vs 25%).
- Earnings and economic status: at age 27, four times as many programme group members as no-programme group members earned $2,000 or more per month (29% vs 7%). Almost three times as many programme group members as no-programme group members owned their own homes (36% vs 13%), and over twice as many owned second cars (30% vs 13%). Three-quarters as many programme group members as no-programme members received welfare assistance or other social services at some time as adults (59% vs 80%).
- Educational performance: one-third again as many programme group members as no-programme group members graduated from regular or adult high school or received General Education Development certification (71% vs 54%).
- Commitment to marriage: although the same percentages of programme males and no-programme males were married (26%), the married programme males were married nearly twice as long as the married no-programme males (averages of 6.2 years and 3.3 years respectively). Five times as many programme females as no-programme females were married at the age-27 interview (40% vs 8%). Programme females had only about two-thirds as many out-of-wedlock births as did no-programme females (57% of births compared to 83% of births).

The High/Scope Preschool Curriculum Comparison Study

Another High/Scope longitudinal study, the High/Scope Preschool Comparison Curriculum Study (Schweinhart, Weikart and Larner, 1986), grew out of the main findings of the Perry Preschool Project and, like the Perry study, produced findings that seem fairly conclusive. This study examined the specific impact of the High/Scope curriculum as compared to two other kinds of curricula: the traditional nursery setting, and a more rigid and formal approach called Distar. Again, subjects were children from poor families, living in Ypsilanti, with IQs ranging from 70 to 85. Forty-one three-year-olds were divided among the three programmes in about equal numbers and went to pre-school for the prescribed two-and-a-half hours a day, five days a week, for two academic years. A teacher made a 90-minute home visit every week.

Each group of children involved in this study experienced distinct kinds of high-quality pre-schooling differentiated primarily by the degree of initiative expected of the child and the teacher. In the first, called Distar, the teacher initiated activities and the child responded to them. Classroom activities were prescribed by behavioural sequences of stimuli, responses and positive reinforcements. In the second, High/Scope, both teacher and child planned and initiated activities and actively worked together. In the third, the traditional nursery, the child initiated and the teacher responded; classroom activities were the teacher's responses to the child's expressed needs and interests, and the teacher encouraged the children to engage actively in free play. All three programmes in the study were part of the same research project, with the same director (Weikart), funding source, personnel policies and position in the school system.

The mean IQ of the children who had attended these three programmes rose a dramatic 27 points during the first year of the programme. The three pre-school groups differed little in their patterns of IQ and school achievement over time. However, according to self-reports at age 15, the group that had attended the Distar pre-school programme engaged in twice as many acts of property violence. The Distar group also reported relatively poor relations with their families, less participation in sports, fewer appointments to school positions, and less reaching out to others for help with personal problems. This comparative study concluded that loosely structured, child-centred programmes which aim to provide children with more than the ability to succeed in typical school settings are better for the child's social/emotional health and well-being in the long-term.

Summarising the research literature

The vast majority of research has shown that pre-school education leads to immediate, measurable gains in educational and social development, and that the benefits are strongest in children from disadvantaged backgrounds. Although all the Consortium studies reported an early rise in the IQ measurement of the children and a subsequent 'wash-out' of these earlier gains within three to four years, the most rigorous studies (especially the Consortium ones) showed that high- quality early education leads to lasting cognitive and social benefits in children which persist throughout adolescence and adulthood.

Woodhead (1985) summarised the findings from this compilation of longitudinal studies as follows:

> This rich set of data shows with remarkable consistency that children who experienced a pre-school programme were less likely to be referred to special education classes or required to repeat a grade; they were more achievement orientated, and their parents had higher educational and occupational aspirations than control children. They also more often completed high school and were more likely to find employment.

Other less conclusive studies (for example, Rice, 1989) remind us to be cautious. Indeed, occasional analyses in the 1970s, such as the Westinghouse study and the studies of Abt Associates, raised questions as to the long-term effectiveness of Headstart (Hodges, 1978). 'We cannot simply inoculate children in one year against the ravages of a life of deprivation.' (Kagan and Zigler, 1987, p.37.).

Others suggest that placing too much emphasis on early education can be negative. According to a report of the Institute for Development of Educational Advancement (IDEA):

> A seven year experience with the CPCs (Child–Parent Center Programs) has demonstrated that short-term programmes cannot replace extensive alternatives in the education of disadvantaged children. In fact, short-term programmes can actually be dangerous in that they pretend to benefits they cannot deliver, causing disenchantment with programmes that might be effective. (Stenner and Mueller, 1973, p.35.)

This suggests that very high-quality pre-schooling must be built upon and consolidated throughout the child's educational career. Linda Meyer's New York City PS137 Headstart Follow Thru Programme is an additional pre-school model which recognises this. This model supplemented the New York City Headstart programme with three or four years of training of children in the primary school. The PS137 study provided two years of pre-school, then kindergarten, and then three years of Follow Thru, and the improvements in reading scores seemed to continue through the seventh grade (Meyer, 1984). Furthermore, there was some evidence of a higher rate of graduation from high school among the children who were exposed to Follow Thru. This study concluded that if children have received a basic grasp of fundamentals by the third grade – and this study carried them through third grade (age approximately nine years) – their chances of later success were considerably greater.

Overall, in their examination of research on the provision of quality pre-school education, Sylva and David (1990) concluded that researchers have been rightly cautious in using the findings from national surveys in the UK to build causal pathways between pre-school provision and later educational or behavioural outcomes: 'We simply do not know yet whether differing patterns of pre-school provision are correlated with different outcomes or actively cause them' (p.64.)

Investigating effectiveness

Why were some programmes more effective than others? In light of the different results from a variety of research studies, the question has to be asked why some programmes produce long-term benefits and others do not. A number of reasons can be offered, but suggestions should be made with caution because, as Melhuish (1993) said, programmes differ not just from each other but also depending on the country in which they are being implemented, and the specific cultural differences to which they are subject. Nonetheless, in the following section possible reasons for the superiority of some programmes over others will be investigated. These include first, quality of the programme, secondly, the particular curriculum employed by a pre-school, thirdly, the emphasis that different curricula place on benefits that are more difficult to quantify, for example, the fostering of positive attitudes, and fourthly, parental involvement.

Quality

So far we have looked at two broad categories of pre-school education – mainstream and compensatory. The quality of mainstream pre-schooling is not always consistent. In the Jowett and Sylva study (1986) which found in favour of local authority nursery education in terms of positive effects on the children in attendance, all the children came from working-class homes. They received pre-school education that varied considerably in terms of quality. The playgroups were poorly resourced and managed by parents working on tight budgets. The nursery schools, on the other hand, were staffed by fully qualified teachers who fostered autonomy, perseverance and academic motivation. Compensatory education programmes can also vary in quality, but many which are government-initiated are well-resourced and openly accountable. The compensatory education studies that we have cited so far included an inbuilt monitoring feature which meant that high-quality, while not assured, was more likely. In general terms, research on compensatory education has tended to concentrate on measurable effects of pre-schooling on the lives of the children, while research on mainstream pre-schooling has focused more on the quality of service provided.

What do we mean by good quality?

Any definition of quality depends upon which values are given priority. Quality can be defined from the perspective of parents, child care workers, employers and children. Many authors (Rumbold, 1990; Pugh, 1992; Elfer and Wedge, 1992) have attempted to define it. Farquhar (1990) in her contribution to the quality debate outlined various perspectives on quality. The *child development perspective* is concerned with the potential effects of children's experiences in an early childhood programme on their intellectual, physical and motor, social and psychological development. The *child's perspective* defines quality in terms of children's perceptions of their experience in the early childhood setting; for example, their likes and dislikes. From the *parent perspective* quality is the extent to which early childhood services meet parents' needs and fulfil their expectations; for example, hours of opening, possible role in influencing programme structure and content. The *staff perspective* defines quality in terms of staff experiences and working conditions; staff levels, staff attitudes and burn-out rates have a significant influence on the quality of children's experiences. The *government or regulatory perspective* views the State as having a social and moral obligation to set national standards and to monitor compliance levels. The *social service perspective* is a concern that early childhood facilities provide a comprehensive care service. The *social policy funding perspective* views quality in relation to social policy and the extent to which the State is financially willing to support the early childhood sector. Lastly, when quality is defined in terms of the social norms, values, customs and beliefs of the people served by an early childhood centre, this is known as a *cultural specific perspective* on quality.

A number of structural aspects contribute to the quality of child care; these include group size, adult–child ratio, caregiver training, stability of caregivers, working conditions for caregivers, equipment and accommodation. These factors are associated with good quality, and when child care settings are well provided for with regard to these structural aspects then good-quality care is likely, although not guaranteed. Often a combination of these structural factors is comparatively easy to measure and usually correlates well with other measures of quality. However, such indices of quality should be regarded as markers rather than actual measures of quality of care. Equally important is the quality of the relationship between the staff and the children, for example if adults are responsive, positive, accepting and informative in their interaction with children (Vernon and Smith, 1994).

The programmes included in the Consortium for Longitudinal Studies were of a high quality in the sense that they had low ratios of staff to children; they were well resourced; they offered planned programmes with carefully directed curricula; the research element brought a high level of professional support to the staff; and all included a weekly home visit of about one-and-a-half hours – a service also available to the control group.

Hence, programmes that fulfil the quality criteria which we have just outlined are more likely to succeed in terms of enhancing both short- and long-term academic and social achievements by children. Programmes which would be rated 'poor' or even 'inconsistent' in terms of possessing quality features are least likely to be beneficial to the children attending.

Curriculum

One question which is often asked is whether the kind of curriculum adopted by a pre-school makes a difference. While educators are more likely to believe in the superiority of the curriculum in which they have been trained and to promote its continued use, research appears to indicate that curricula, be they Montessori-based, High/Scope, Steiner, or Schema-based are similar in their short-term effects so long as they are consistently of a high quality. Indeed, it is interesting that the Early Childhood Education Forum Early Years Curriculum Project is currently working together for a national framework for early education in England and Wales. Given the promotion of the High/Scope curriculum, this question of superiority of one curriculum over another is of particular interest. Within the Consortium studies, a range of curricula and teaching styles were employed; this, in itself, did not appear to be a significant variable in terms of benefits to the children, since all the programmes were high-quality, employing well-planned and structured curricula with an emphasis on cognitive development. Indeed, the later Preschool Comparison Curriculum study by Schweinhart, Weikart and Larner (1986), which was discussed earlier, has been subject to methodological criticisms (Bereiter, 1986; Gersten, 1986). For instance Bereiter felt that the level of delinquency at age 15 of those receiving the direct instruction curriculum could reasonably be explained by the unequal demographics – the high proportion of males and those without parental supervision in the direct-instruction sample. Gersten highlighted other weaknesses; for example, the use of an extremely liberal level of significance was thought to be inappropriate, data on achievement and school attendance were omitted, the three pre-school curriculum groups differed little in their patterns of IQ and school achievement over time.

Hence we cannot state that the specifics of the actual curriculum employed by any pre-school are a significant factor in terms of positive gains for the child. Only in pre-schools where curricula differ in terms of the quality features we have already mentioned are there differential effects on the children.

Attitude change

Some programmes may be more effective than others as a result of the positive attitudes that they foster in children, rather than in terms of directly measurable effects such as increases in IQ. The High/Scope Preschool Curriculum Comparison Study described above is one example. Some children are by nature more likely to develop negative feelings about themselves and their abilities than others. Obviously, this has a large effect on their functioning, both cognitive and emotional. Indeed, Dweck and Leggett (1988) studied children's explanations of academic success and failure and concluded that there are two main categories into which children fall – mastery-oriented and helpless. In their study, mastery-oriented children apparently maintained a positive orientation to a task designed to prompt failure, and continued to employ problem-solving strategies. Helpless children showed a marked decline in problem-solving effort. These children appeared to view their difficulties as signs of their low ability; they rarely engaged in self-monitoring or self-instruction. However, many psychologists feel that children younger than Dweck and Leggett's sample also strive for mastery. According to Heyman, Dweck and Cain (1992), vulnerability to teacher criticism is evident from the earliest years at school. High/Scope is one programme which affords much importance to fostering mastery in the child, primarily through encouraging active learning and independence, as will be discussed in Chapter 3; this may be one of the most important reasons why it has been found to improve the life chances of children (Sylva, 1994b).

Lazar and others (1982), in their review of the effects of the 11 Consortium studies, felt that:

> Perhaps early education taught the children some concrete cognitive skills and also exposed them to some school-relevant non-cognitive skills such as attentiveness to teachers, ability to follow instructions, and task perseverance. When the children entered the first grade they had positive attitudes towards classroom activities, were able to adapt to classroom procedures, and were able to learn and do the school work. The public school experience, in short, was positive. The children's positive attitudes towards school were reinforced; they felt competent. In all probability their teachers identified them as competent and treated them as such. Once set in motion success tended to breed success... (Lazar and others, 1982.)

Furthermore they constructed a theoretical model to explain their findings which hypothesised that increased parental expectations and positive attitudes served to motivate their children.

Schweinhart and Weikart agreed that attitude change was the most important factor contributing to their findings; the research data suggested that both children and their parents were more achievement orientated and had increased aspirations for their future:

> The essential process connecting early childhood experience to patterns of improved success in school and the community seemed to be the development of habits, traits, and dispositions that allowed the child to interact positively with other people and with tasks. This process was based neither on permanently improved intellectual performance nor on academic knowledge. (Schweinhart and Weikart, 1993, p.4.)

Berreuta-Clement and colleagues (1984) suggested that pre-school education promotes cognitive and social skills that result in greater school readiness and a smoother transition to school. Children leave the nursery 'ready to learn' and are easily recognised by teachers who show positive expectations and treatment, and this, in turn, fosters improved student attitudes towards school and better school behaviour (called 'school commitment' by Weikart and colleagues). These serve as protective factors against the later risk of maladjustment and delinquency. Schweinhart and Weikart argued that well-resourced, cognitively oriented pre-school programmes such as High/Scope should be effective outside the original setting in which the research took place. Similarly, Sylva sees the most lasting impact of early education as children's aspirations for education and employment, their motivations and commitment to school. These are not moulded directly through experiences in the pre-school classroom but are indirect effects of children entering schools with a learning orientation and beginning a 'pupil career' with confidence (Sylva, 1992). This enables them to avoid early school failure and placement in special education, two critical markers that constitute major turning-points in the lives of many children according to Maughan (1988: cited in Sylva, 1994a). Weissberg, Caplan and Harwood (1991: cited in Sylva, 1994a) felt that early childhood education may be viewed as an innovative mental health strategy that affects many risk and protective factors.

The message seems to be then that the effects of pre-school are not always directly observable or quantifiable. Pre-school education may indeed change the lives of young children; it appears to do this by fostering positive attitudes, and inspiring motivation and a healthy need for achievement. This in turn allows the child a sense of control and responsibility in his or her own life, crucial factors in the development of self-worth and self-esteem.

Involving Parents

A further variable in the evaluation of pre-school services is the extent to which parents are involved. What exactly do we mean by parental involvement? Pugh and de'Ath (1989) developed a typology to describe levels of parental involvement in services for families with children under five years. Their typology ranges from non-participation, through support, participation to partnership and finally control. The case in favour of working together with parents is made on two grounds:

- partnership is valuable in itself as it leads to personal growth, self-esteem and empowerment;
- partnership is essential to the functional success of the service, for example the Portage model of intervention.

The message from some of the intervention projects with 'disadvantaged' families has been that the project's impact on children lasted longer when their parents were also involved. Indeed, in the 1970s Bronfenbrenner's longitudinal research (1976) on the effectiveness of early education concluded that early intervention was effective but only if intervention is family, rather than child-centred. David (1990) observed that early pioneers such as Margaret McMillan had stressed the importance of the parental role and the relationships between parents and the school. Not everyone agrees though; White, Taylor and Moss (1992) examined the belief that early intervention programmes that involve parents are more effective than those that do not. They found no convincing evidence and concluded that much of the perception that parent involvement is beneficial has been based on anecdotal reports and poorly designed research. They suggested that in the future carefully designed research should help us to balance our hopes with reality.

Overall, though, there is general agreement in the literature to support the view that participation by parents in the development and education of themselves and their children, is a positive and perhaps necessary force. How that participation evolves and how the child/parent/professional/community benefit are issues that require further research if parental involvement is to develop a sound theoretical base.

Conclusion

While one year of early childhood education has value for its own sake, it is not the kind of response to poverty that makes a significant contribution to its elimination (Ramey, 1985). Unless combined with other changes, such programmes are not likely to make a significant impact. Most studies suggest that, at best, these early childhood one-year pre-kindergarten programmes have a short-term impact on children in terms of fewer retentions in grade, fewer needs for special education, more positive attitudes among the children or among their parents towards achievement. Fuerst and Fuerst conclude that many programme approaches have to be tried. There is no national programme that can be applied everywhere. Children's developmental needs vary as they grow. What we really need is a galaxy of long-term programmes with careful selection of staff and heavy parental involvement.

An analysis of the research indicates that programmes most likely to succeed in preparing children for school are those which emphasise both cognitive and social skills; where staff support and encourage and are flexible in their approach, where parents are involved and integral to the curriculum; programmes that are rooted in local culture and traditions, which understand the central role of women and support them in their many tasks; and those which recognise the need for a holistic approach – in other words 'good-quality' curricula. The High/Scope curriculum offers such a framework for high-quality early years education and is the one whose value and effects, in practice, we shall be assessing in this study.

2. Education in Ireland

This chapter is made up of three sections. In the first, an attempt is made to familiarise the reader with early childhood services in Ireland, specifically the extent and type of provision. In the second, the primary school structure in Ireland is examined; we look at responsibility for primary schools and their funding. In the third section, the relationship between education and poverty is explored to emphasise how essential education is if disadvantaged children are to be helped to break out of the poverty cycle. The extent of poverty in Ireland and what this means for Irish school-children (and also school-leavers) is investigated.

Early childhood services in Ireland

In the past 20 years there has been a growth in early childhood services in Ireland. This is due to a variety of influences. First was the impact of the Headstart movement in the USA in the late 1960s (see page 13) which promoted the advantage of intervention through pre-school provision to disadvantaged children. This was accompanied by a growth of interest in the early play, educational and social needs of young children which, in turn, gave rise to the playgroup and naíonra (Irish-speaking playgroup) movement. Furthermore, the demographic trend that has emerged in recent years – the increase in participation in the workforce by both parents – has led not only to child care becoming a political issue in relation to equal opportunities for women, but also to the proliferation of the various child care arrangements which were outlined in Chapter 1.

In addition to these factors, there have also been a number of other international and national developments which may have had an influence on early childhood services in Ireland. These include:

- The Summit on Children in 1990, at which the Taoiseach (Irish

Prime Minister) indicated the intention of the Irish government to ratify the United Nations Convention on the Rights of the Child. This was subsequently ratified in September 1992.

- The European Council which agreed the Recommendation on Child Care in March 1992. In effect this meant a recommendation that initiatives be taken in member states to enable women and men to reconcile their occupational, family and upbringing responsibilities arising from the care of children. As a result, child care services should be provided while parents are working, following a course of education or seeking a job. There should be special leave for employed persons with responsibility for the care and upbringing of children. The environment, structure and organisation of work should be made responsive to the needs of workers with children. All member states are expected to meet the criteria outlined in the proposal and should inform the Commission within three years of the measures taken in their state to give effect to the Recommendation.

- The Child Care Act which was signed into law in July 1991. This Act is concerned with the care and protection of children (particularly those at risk) and the regulation of that care and protection both in the family of origin and beyond. One part deals with pre-school provision – for example, issues such as securing the safety and promoting the development of children attending pre-school services. The Government is committed to full implementation of this Act by the end of 1996.

- The Programme for Economic and Social Progress (PESP) which acknowledges the needs of children and particularly those coming from the more disadvantaged sectors of our society.

- The first ministerial appointment in 1992 specifically relating to children, with a Minister of State at the Department of Health taking special responsibility for the coordination of services.

Although these developments are obviously positive, much remains to be done in order to improve the quality of child care services available in Ireland. Hayes (1992) highlighted two contemporary issues relating to these developments. The first concerns the focus of the services. She noted:

> While welcoming the various factors that have led to an increased focus on the subject, I believe that at times the child and the needs of the child may have taken second place to other driving principles such as the provision of a service to parents. This can be accounted for to

some extent by the ad hoc and unregulated development of the services. (p.2 para. 1.)

Secondly Hayes warned against complacency, despite substantial developments in the area of early childhood care. She pointed out:

> There is a danger that we may become complacent in the light of the developments in Ireland over the last twenty years and I want to nudge at that complacency to point out that the discipline of early childhood care and education has received very little attention in general and virtually none where it matters most – at a policy level. For example, we have yet to hear any government debate about, let alone to satisfy, the UN Convention and our Child Care Act has been only partially implemented and funded.... Furthermore, we live in a country with a high proportion of children in poverty, and a growing number of lone parents who need support in many areas, not least in the area of early childhood services. (ibid p.2 para. 3.)

Pre-school services in Ireland: the level of provision

So what is the level of provision of early-years services in Ireland? As in Britain, pre-school child care services in Ireland are limited in their provision. If we compare the statistics on the number of young children receiving publicly funded day care services in the countries in the then European Community (see Table 2.1), we see that Ireland is below the average but not as low as Britain or the lowest provider, Portugal. (McKenna, 1988.)

Table 2.1 Publicly funded pre-school provision in EU member states

Country (Population in millions)	0–2 years %	3–school age %
Germany (61)	3	60+
France (55)	23	95
Italy (57)	5	88
Netherlands (15)*	9	75
Belgium (10)	23	95
Luxembourg (0.4)	1–	55
UK (57)	2–	44
Ireland (3.5)	1–	55
Denmark (5)**	44	87
Greece (10)	2.5	62
Portugal (10)	4	25
Spain (39)	5+	66

*3–4 years; **3–6 years; all other 3–5 years
From: *Child Care and Equal Opportunities*, McKenna, 1988

Comparatively low as these figures for Ireland are, they tend to overestimate the provision of services designed specifically for younger (under-five) children. Unlike other European countries Ireland has very little nursery education directly geared to meeting the needs of children under five. In contrast, Ireland has a tradition of offering places in national schools to children before they reach the statutory age. Indeed, it was estimated that, in 1989, 55.7 per cent of four-year-olds and 99 per cent of five- to seven-year-olds were receiving full-time education at primary school (Gilligan, 1991). However, Hayes believes the figure of 55.7 per cent of four-year-olds is an underestimate; she regards 75 per cent as a more appropriate figure. While this may appear to offer the advantage of an early structured input, such services are often inappropriate for the under-fives, not least in the ratio of staff to children and the over-academic approach to learning. When compared with other OECD countries, the Republic of Ireland has the largest pupil–teacher ratio at pre-primary level. In fact, over 50 per cent are in classes of more than 30 children with one teacher (Hayes, 1992).

No national policy exists to coordinate pre-school education. As a result, Ireland has great diversity in its pre-school provision both in nature and source. As was acknowledged in Chapter 1, whether pre-schooling is provided by the public or private sector is reflected to a large extent by the type of child (in terms of socio-economic background) who attends. It is difficult to estimate what percentage of children attending services is likely to be disadvantaged, but of the 7,263 children aided by the health boards, it can be assumed that most are to some degree disadvantaged (Hayes, 1992).

Pre-school services: the providers

Who provides early childhood services in Ireland? We look at public and private sector provision in turn.

Public sector provision

There exists a division of responsibility between the departments of Health and Education with regard to early childhood services. Under the terms of the Child Care Act (1991), responsibilities in relation to pre-schools lie with the Minister for Health. Section 50 of the Act provides that the Minister will consult with the Minister for Education who will advise on the educational aspects of provision governing pre-schooling.

Department of Health: under the 1970 Health Act the Department of Health is empowered through the Health Boards to provide grants towards the operating costs of centres catering for children in need of special support or for families needing support. The bulk of this support goes to voluntary bodies who provide a number of day centres throughout the country.

Department of Education: in addition to children attending infant classes of primary schools, the Department of Education supports a number of early education projects for young disadvantaged children. For example:

- The Rutland Street Project established in 1969 to cater for three- to five-year-olds living in a particularly disadvantaged part of Dublin city.
- The Department has also partially funded the developing pre-school services for Travellers; there are over 40 such pre-schools catering for over 400 pre-school children of Traveller families.
- In 1990 the Department launched the Home/School Liaison Project which provides full-time locally based coordinators to groups of schools in areas of particular disadvantage. Though not exclusively concerned with early years experience, the coordinators establish links with pre-schools and with voluntary and statutory groups in their area.
- In 1994, the Minister for Education announced details of Early Start. This pre-school programme allowed for the establishment of pre-school centres located in areas designated as disadvantaged. All the pre-school centres are closely linked with a national school in each designated area. A high level of parental involvement is encouraged, with parents involved in the day-to-day organising and running of the unit and participating with their children in unit activities, as well as having strong representation on an advisory group in each unit.

It is not possible to get an accurate report of the number of children under six attending Department of Education services; however, the figures attending infant classes and the special projects in 1991 came to 126,210 children (Hayes, 1992).

Private sector provision

This takes the form of playgroups, naíonraí and Montessori Schools. Almost 21,000 children attend playgroups throughout Ireland. Eighty-five per cent of these are home playgroups and the remaining 15 per cent are community-based. The latter are non-profit making and receive some support from the Department of Health through the Health Boards. *An Comhcoiste Reamhscolaiochta Teo* organise and support a system of Irish-speaking playgroups, the naíonraí. There are 218 naíonraí in the 26 counties and they cater for some 2,500 children. As with the playgroups, a proportion of the children attending naíonraí are supported through the local Health Boards. There are approximately 139 Montessori Schools catering for almost 1,700 children (Hayes 1992). McKenna estimated that, in 1988, approximately 2,500 children up to six years old were attending private and workplace nurseries, many of which provided an educational component in the form of a morning pre-school session for the three- to five-year-olds.

Primary school structure in Ireland

Primary schooling in Ireland shares many of the irregularities and inconsistencies of pre-primary education. In fact the Republic is probably unique among European countries in the degree to which it administers an education system without a comprehensive and up-to-date legislative structure and no overall Education Act (*Education for a Changing World: Green Paper on Education*, Department of Education (Republic), 1992, p.31).

Compulsory education in Ireland extends from six to 15 years. Parents may choose where their child goes to school (subject to availability of places). There is no charge for attendance at national schools and in all but a minority of secondary schools. However, the shortfall that can arise between grant-aid and actual running costs may mean that in many schools there is a strong emphasis on fund-raising and possibly even on voluntary contributions by parents. Only two per cent of schools are run privately (fees are charged and the school receives no state funds). There are 3,261 state-funded primary national schools and they are almost all under denominational control, with 93.2 per cent under the patronage of the local Roman Catholic bishop (Dail, Irish Government Debates, 1988).

Two major exceptions to this denominational pattern are the ten model national schools run directly by the State, and the small but growing multi-denominational sector, whose schools are under the direct control of parents and supporters (Gilligan, 1991). Another development regarding primary school provision has been the establishment of 62 Gaelscoileanna (Irish-speaking schools) by September 1989. These schools, recognised by the Department of Education, are located outside the Gaeltacht regions (areas where Irish is the primary language). Indeed demand has often been strongest in urban working-class areas, not traditionally the stronghold of active supporters of the Irish language. In the present study which is conducted in a particularly disadvantaged part of Dublin, out of a total sample of 15 schools, two (13.3 per cent) are Irish-speaking and are attended by four of the total sample group of 40 children.

Up until 1975, schools were managed by the local parish priest (or his equivalent in other denominations) who was himself appointed by the local bishop (or his equivalent). In 1975, boards of management were introduced at the behest of the Department of Education. In schools of six teachers or fewer, a board consists of three nominees of the patrons, two representatives elected by parents and the principal. In larger schools, the patron nominates four members, parents elect two, teachers one and the principal also has a place (Gilligan, 1991). This structure gives the appearance of democratising primary education, but in reality little has changed. Teachers are appointed by these boards and their names are then forwarded to the Department of Education for ratification and subsequent confirmation.

Levels of funding available to the national schools system mean that many children attend large classes: two out of three children in national schools are in classes of 30 or more. Lack of funding also influences the number of posts available to supplement the resources of schools where there are concentrations of children with a need for remedial education. During 1990 there were approximately 890 remedial teachers serving in the region of 1,100 national schools (Primary Education Review Body, 1990). A very limited school psychological service is now being introduced into the primary school sector. In recent years, two schemes have operated to bring extra resources to national schools in disadvantaged areas. One offers financial assistance, for example grants for books and equipment, special in-service training for teachers, and promotes home–school liaison. The second offers additional teaching posts and benefits 181 schools out of a total of more than 3,200 national schools (Primary Education Review Body, 1990).

The primary school curriculum is set by the Department centrally, and while a certain latitude is allowed – especially in more disadvantaged areas – teachers are required to adhere to this curriculum.

Education and social disadvantage

The extent of social disadvantage

Social disadvantage in Ireland is a countrywide problem, most visible and probably most severe in inner cities and large local authority housing developments (such as Tallaght, the location of this research study). While it is difficult to define what exactly is meant by the term 'disadvantage', family poverty and failure to benefit from the education system are key indicators of this state. The incidence of both of these problems in Ireland is substantial:

- approximately one-third of the population has an income which is less than 60 per cent of the average household income;
- 31.4 per cent of the general population and about 40 per cent of young people aged under 14 years live in poverty, if the threshold for poverty is set at that point where household income falls below 60 per cent of average household income (Callan and others, 1989);
- up to 8,000 young people (about 12 per cent of the age cohort) leave school every year without a formal qualification or with what is generally regarded as a poor qualification;
- in some areas of poverty more than one-quarter of those leaving primary schools have been found to have serious literacy and numeracy problems or to be in need of remedial help.

Children from poor families are at a distinct disadvantage in terms of the education system. From the research evidence it is clear that lack of education plays an indirect but important part in the perpetuation of poverty. Indeed the effects of poverty have, to a very significant extent, occurred before children leave primary school:

> Poor children are more likely than non-poor children to be low-achievers in school, to repeat one or two grades and to eventually drop out of school. They are more likely to engage in delinquent and criminal behaviour, to become unmarried teen parents and to be welfare-dependent; they are also likely to earn less if they are employed. (National Centre for Children in Poverty, 1990, p.56, cited in Carta, 1991.)

The nature of educational disadvantage

The term 'educational disadvantage' refers to a concept which over the last 30 years has been used to explain why children from poor backgrounds do not derive the same benefit from their schooling as children from more comfortable backgrounds. Underlying the concept of disadvantage is the idea that there exists a difference between the school and non-school experiences of children who are poor. As a result of a variety of factors in their environment, disadvantaged children develop characteristics which make transition to school difficult and which impede progress. These include inadequate housing conditions, poor nourishment and diet, lack of opportunities to avail themselves of out-of-school educational experiences, and the absence, in their immediate environment, of people who have benefited from the education system and who could serve as role models. Furthermore, the school environment possesses a variety of characteristics (related, for example, to the type of language used and to aspects of the curriculum or the overall ethos) which represent impediments to the adjustment of children from these backgrounds. Indeed, the way society is structured in general means that those living in poverty are deprived of opportunities to participate fully in controlling their own lives and shaping their own futures.

Furthermore, parents' perceptions of schools may be coloured by their own experience of school, which in the case of those who are disadvantaged was typically unfavourable. Thus, while parents of disadvantaged children may recognise the importance of schooling in general, they do not expect that school will be of benefit to their children. This attitude, although probably not directly acknowledged, obviously affects the more subtle messages that parents convey (albeit unwittingly) to their children. As a result, since the mid-1980s, some writers on the topic of educational disadvantage have tended to concentrate on the societal causes of the problem and have advocated strategies which seek to empower parents to exercise more control over their lives, particularly by becoming more actively involved in the education of their own children (Widlake, 1986; Woodhead and McGrath, 1988).

The relationship between the lack of educational attainment and subsequent unemployment, and the role of inequality in this relationship, has attracted considerable attention in recent years. A report which examined social mobility in the Republic of Ireland for the Economic and Social Research Institute concluded that we are confronted not simply with a minority of disadvantaged children and schools who have obvious social problems but, rather, with a wider problem, posed by the vast majority of working-class children who achieve significantly below their potential. Furthermore, the class barriers which lead to underachievement do not diminish as one moves beyond the primary level (Whelan and Whelan, 1984).

Measured performance of disadvantaged children

Disadvantaged children perform relatively poorly on IQ tests, even when such tests are administered at a young age. However, in the opinion of Rohwer (1971) and Colman (1987), this relatively poor performance is more likely to be due to lack of exposure to the kinds of tasks and materials that make up the test than a lack of facility for learning. Furthermore, in formal settings such as schools, socio-economically disadvantaged children have been found to use language in less elaborate forms and for less complex purposes than do middle-class children. However, this may be due more to situational constraints than to lack of linguistic capacity. Several studies (Houston, 1970; Labov, 1969; Tizard and others, 1983) have shown that in relaxed, informal settings disadvantaged children employ elaborate and internally consistent language structures for a whole range of cognitive and social purposes. There is also evidence, from the area of linguistics, which shows that it is more accurate to view the speech of disadvantaged people as a variety of English, which is different from but not necessarily inferior to, the variety used by middle-class people (Edwards, 1989).

Outcomes of educational disadvantage

There are several ways to measure the outcomes of educational disadvantage. One method is to analyse the annual school-leavers' surveys (see, for instance, Breen, 1984; Hannan, 1986; Youth Employment Agency, 1986). In one of these analyses Hannan showed that young people who leave school without achieving at least five Ds on the Leaving Certificate are disadvantaged, to varying degrees, in terms of labour-force participation. Combining data received in 1984 and 1985, Hannan arrived at an estimate of 23 per cent of boys and 17 per cent of girls whose schooling has left them poorly equipped to compete in the labour market. While the numbers remaining in school to Senior Cycle have increased and the numbers leaving during Junior Cycle have decreased since then (Department of Labour, 1991), and overall 90 per cent of 16–year-olds are in full-time education, it seems that this figure may mask severe dropout rates in some schools serving socio-economically disadvantaged areas (Department of Education (1994) *School Attendance/Truancy Report*). For example, in the North Inner City of Dublin, 44 per cent of the population left school before the age of 15 (McKeown, 1991).

The link between education and poverty

While equality of access to education exists to the age of 15 (the official school-leaving age) it would appear that the goals of equality of attainment, regardless of socio-economic background and ability, are not taken seriously in Irish education. Indeed, it has been argued that the educational system functions as the primary mechanism by which social inequalities are reproduced in Irish society (Breen and others, 1990). Early school-leavers (those finishing before the Leaving Certificate) and dropouts (those finishing without any qualifications), who are the most seriously disadvantaged, come predominantly from lower-income groups.

Staying on at school has serious implications for employment prospects. The unemployment rate among those who obtain a Leaving Certificate is about one-third the rate for those who leave school without any certification, and about half the rate for those who leave with a Group or Intermediate Certificate (Breen, 1991). Educational qualifications, a major determinant of employment prospects, are closely related to the socio-economic status of the family. For example, virtually all students from professional/managerial backgrounds obtain a Leaving Certificate and nearly half of them go on to third-level colleges (Breen, 1984; Clancy, 1988). Hence, children who are poor seem destined to remain poor and marginalised in the future, unless specific policies aimed at reversing the situation are adopted and are successful.

Compensatory education in the pre-school years

Having looked at the extent and causes of social and educational disadvantage experienced by Irish children, in this final section we will review attempts to alleviate this distress.

The rationale behind intervening in the early years of a child's life (especially the period between three and five years old) is so disadvantaged children and their families can be prepared for the transition to school, thereby affecting some of the problems associated with that transition. In Chapter 1, compensatory pre-school education programmes were discussed in detail. The research evidence indicates that involvement in good-quality pre-schooling results in improved school performance in the short term. In most studies, the observed benefits tended to reduce or disappear in the early years of formal schooling. However, several follow-up studies have indicated that the benefits of pre-schooling reappear in later years. The 'sleeper effect' suggests that the effects of early intervention on the child's cognitive processes remain dormant until triggered by new demands in the young person's life (Lewin, 1977). As discussed in Chapter 1, it is still not clear whether it is the pre-school experience itself or other factors associated with the pre-school experience that are responsible for these benefits. Furthermore, there is evidence that, in some circumstances, the existence of various kinds of early educational provision can act as a catalyst for other developments which enhance the quality of life in the community by empowering parents and others. Pre-schools can trigger a cycle of interactive changes not only in the children, but in their relationship to their family and school, and in turn to the wider social context in which they are gaining competence (Woodhead, 1985).

To date, little research has been carried out on pre-school provision in Ireland. Of the studies that have been undertaken, the 'Rutland Street Project', referred to in Chapter 1 (see page 11), is the best-known. This pre-school project developed a special curriculum for its children, and was designed to involve parents by means of home-visits and parent–teacher meetings. Longitudinal follow-up indicated that, on most of the measures, little or no difference was found between the group which had participated in the pre-school programme and the group which had not in terms of the extent of assignment to special classes, rates of absenteeism and truancy from school (Kellaghan and Greaney, 1992). The early work-experiences of the two groups were also similar, as was the incidence of social deviance and delinquency. There were, however, important long-term differences between the two groups in two key areas. First, programme participants were between two and three times more likely to take public examinations (Intermediate and Group Certificate) than members of the control group. Second, while none of the control group completed second-level education (that is, to Leaving Certificate level), ten per cent of the programme participants did.

One other education programme aimed at increasing the life chances of disadvantaged children that has recently been evaluated is the St Audeon's Parent/Child Health Promotion Project (Hayes and McCarthy, 1992). The pre-school, located in a primary school building in the south inner city of Dublin, provides the opportunity for parental involvement through a parent rota scheme and a parent meeting schedule, drawn up in consultation with parents. Qualitative data suggests that it is achieving some success as past parents are still actively involved in the project, and the school is the only one in the inner city where attendance is on the increase. An evaluation was conducted in early 1993 (O'Flaherty and others, 1994); this consisted of a follow-up of all the children who had attended the pre-school since its inception in 1987 (it was possible to trace approximately 83 per cent of the children involved). Performance of the group on IQ, reading tests and assessments of social/emotional functioning as made by class teachers were evaluated and compared (for each class group) to two other groups of children, one of which had no pre-school experience and another which had 'other' pre-school experience. With regard to social/emotional functioning and reading ability, significant differences between the three groups were found to exist for junior infants level children only, in favour of both pre-school groups. Analysis of scores obtained on a measure of cognitive ability (first to fourth classes only) revealed no significant differences between groups.

Hence, while there are no specific outcomes that can be directly attributed to pre-school, it would appear that the provision of early years education does make some difference to children's performance at school in the early years. Furthermore, although it would seem logical to compare the Irish findings with those from the American research, there are a number of factors which warrant caution in the interpretation of available research. For example, it is important to remember that there are often many differences between the circumstances of disadvantaged children in this country, in terms of the extent of poverty suffered, and those who participated in the projects reported in the American research.

Conclusion

In conclusion, the provision of early childhood education in Ireland is limited and patchy, with a large percentage of under-fives receiving early education in the infant classes of primary schools. This is not an ideal situation as primary schools are not generally equipped to provide the educational input that is appropriate to this age-group. Unfortunately, the provision of pre-school education services to date has often been on an 'ad hoc' basis, as no national policy exists to coordinate pre-primary education. Similar to the situation in the UK, poor levels of funding mean that children attend large classes and only a very limited school psychological service exists for the primary sector. Although there is no direct causal link between educational failure and poverty, a much lower proportion of pupils from working-class or disadvantaged backgrounds sit the Leaving Certificate or reach the standards necessary to enter third level education.

3. What does High/Scope mean?

In this chapter we examine more closely the components of the High/Scope curriculum. We ask what it is that makes High/Scope unique in the world of pre-school education by comparing and contrasting High/Scope with other well-known curricula. Further, we outline the manner in which High/Scope came to be introduced to Britain and Ireland, why Barnardo's – a child care charity dealing primarily with children who are vulnerable and at risk – became interested in High/Scope and the implications of this.

The High/Scope curriculum

The High/Scope curriculum, which has been developed over a period of almost 30 years, draws on the work of a number of experts in the field of child development, for example Piaget and Smilansky. As a result the curriculum is based on well-understood concepts but, as has been remarked: 'a recipe can be unique without having any unfamiliar ingredients' (Langdown, 1989). So, what are these ingredients? Each of the main components of the High/Scope approach are considered below.

Active learning

Active learning means learning that is initiated by the learner, such that it is carried out by the learner rather than simply handed or transmitted to him or her. The belief, based in part on Piaget's theories of child-development, is that mental and physical activity are inextricably related and that children's mental progress is facilitated by their physical interaction with the environment.

> Active learning – the direct and immediate experiencing of objects, people and events – is a necessary condition for cognitive restructuring and hence for development; put simply, young children learn concepts through self-initiated activity. (Hohmann, Banet and Weikart, 1979, p.3.)

This criteria for active learning should be evident throughout all parts of the daily routine. For children to be active learners, they must be allowed to choose and manipulate readily available materials and be encouraged to talk about them. Adults must support and extend children's activities and encourage their cooperation and problem-solving.

Key experiences:

Implicit in the High/Scope concept of active learning are the key experiences, a feature which is at the heart of the High/Scope curriculum. Key experiences occur naturally for children and quite simply they may be described as what children do. They are not goals, nor can they be taught. Fifty key experiences have been identified and grouped into five clusters: (i) *using language*: for example, describing objects, events and relationships; (ii) *active learning*: for example, manipulating, transforming and combining materials; (iii) *representing ideas and experiences*: for example, role-playing, pretending; (iv) *developing logical reasoning*: for example, learning to label, sort and match objects; (v) *understanding time and space*: for example, recalling and anticipating events, learning to locate objects in the classroom. The list is not fixed and has been modified and extended by pre-school educators since the 1960s. The most recent version of Key Experiences is included as an appendix to this chapter.

Key experiences provide the framework for planning and evaluating activities; they enable staff to guide children from one learning experience to another; they suggest questions to put to the children; they enable staff to assess a child's development; they provide a basis for discussing the child with the parent. A teaching team can start the planning process by selecting key experiences they feel are the most appropriate for particular children, for example a child whose language needs attention will be afforded key experiences in using language. Staff may concentrate on getting him or her to express his or her feelings in words, or to describe events that have happened to him or her. They may provide opportunities for having fun with language, for example, introducing nursery rhymes, poems and stories. The team can use the key experiences not only to guide their observations and assessments of children, but also to generate activities and teaching strategies. By concentrating or observing one or two key experiences at a time, staff generally have a better understanding of how most children function in those areas. The following examples may illustrate what is meant by a 'key experience' and how adults might use them within the High/Scope curriculum.

Example 1

In an activity, children choose grades of sandpaper with different textures. Ongoing conversation throughout the activity indicates the children's desire to talk about the textures. The key experiences reflected in their conversation relate to classification and seriation. The adult listens to the children's comments about the differences in textures and encourages them to describe how one sheet is different from another.

Example 2

In another situation, a child notices that she and a member of staff are wearing denim jeans. The adult and child tour the building to see and count who else is wearing denims. Next, they look for people wearing other items of clothing, for example, corduroys and skirts, and then they make a chart to illustrate their findings. Here, the child is classifying clothing according to texture, while the teacher supports and encourages this learning.

Daily routine

The daily routine provides children and adults with a supportive, consistent framework in which to work. Hohmann (Hohmann, Banet and Weikart, 1979) believes that a consistent daily routine frees both adults and children from worrying about or having to decide what comes next, which enables them to use their creative energies on the tasks at hand. The daily routine is designed to accomplish three major goals: first, it provides a sequence of plan/do/review which gives children a process to help them explore, design and carry out activities and make decisions in their learning. Second, it provides for many types of interaction – small and large groups, adult to child, child to child, and also in terms of adult teamwork – and times when activities are child-initiated and adult-initiated. Third, it provides time to work in a variety of environments – inside, outside, on field trips, in various work areas. The daily routine is an essential part of the High/Scope curriculum, but the High/Scope Institute would also say that it is essential that the High/Scope daily routine is used in the context of a supportive framework, and *not* as a management strait-jacket.

Plan/do/review

The crucial element of the High/Scope routine is the *plan/do/ review* sequence: children plan an activity, carry it out and then recall – or, as they become older, evaluate – what they have done. This child-centred approach ensures that the children are making choices and taking decisions about what they will do, with the adults playing a guiding and supporting role. Essentially, during the planning time, a group consisting of the same adults and children meet together to talk about what each child wants to do, and how he or she can go about it. The adult encourages the child to verbalize and hence clarify what he or she wants to do. Usually the child will plan a starting activity and then make a subsequent plan, or plans. Hence, although planning time is a designated time, the planning process can continue throughout work time. As the year progresses, however, some children learn to make more complete and complex initial plans. The advantage of planning is that children who plan for themselves can see that they can make things happen. Hence children experience control over their own activities.

Learning how to plan does not happen immediately. Children must become familiar with the materials that are available, with the names of the work areas, with the names of other people in the room. They will begin by making choices. Initially a child may not understand what a 'plan' means, but in time the connection between the choice and the chosen activity will be made. Children may indicate their plans in a variety of ways – by gesturing to certain materials, by pointing to certain areas in the room, or by verbally describing in an increasingly detailed manner, what they have in mind. When planning is finished, children begin to 'do'.

'Doing' or work time is the longest single time period in the daily routine, lasting for at least an hour. This ensures that children have time to persist, concentrate and follow their plans through. Work time gives children the opportunity to organise and to act, to decide which materials, tools and equipment are best for their purposes and to develop the skills necessary to use them with ease. For adults, work time is a time to observe and learn what interests the children and how they perceive and solve problems, to take cues from the children and work along with them, and to support, encourage and extend children's ideas (Hohmann, Banet and Weikart, 1979).

Reviewing basically gives children the opportunity to remember and recall to the adult and the group what they did during work time. Children remember what they did in a variety of ways by talking about their actions, showing something they used at work time, drawing pictures or even miming what they did. Like the planning process, review may happen spontaneously during work time, as children complete what they have set out to do. Reviewing helps children see the relationship between their plans and their work and indeed the work and its outcome. It gives children the opportunity to reflect on what they have been doing. It also gives them ideas based on each others' experiences. Instead of following an adult's prescribed instructions, if a child plans his or her own activity, works with support but not under direction, and recalls and reviews the experience, then this is a very active experience. It is in this way that the core of the High/Scope philosophy, active learning, is actually put into practice. Active learning empowers children, it gives them a sense of responsibility that other curricula often fall short on. As we mentioned in Chapter 1, planning may be associated with the emergence of mastery, and as such is linked to the development of positive attitudes. Sylva feels that the explicit way in which the teacher uses the plan/do/review cycle within High/Scope encourages a mastery orientation. 'Perhaps the plan/do/review cycle is the cause of greater autonomy, commitment and aspirations seen by graduates of the High/Scope programmes demonstrated to be cost effective.' (Sylva, 1994b, p.94.)

While the plan/do/review sequence forms the most significant part of the daily routine, there are other important elements – time for small groups, tidy-up time, circle time, outside time and time for snacks.

Small-group time

During small-group time the adult works with a group of up to 13 children for 15 to 20 minutes. Hence, adult-initiated activity time is much shorter than child-initiated time (which takes at least one hour). The adult initiates activities which are based on his or her observations of the children's interests, helps them obtain materials and provides appropriate support. Children participate actively, use their own set of materials, solve problems, cooperate and interact with peers.

Each adult works with the same small group of children over a period of time. This has to be a sufficiently long enough period for the adults and children to get to know each other well. Because they know exactly who they are going to work with from day to day, the children feel secure. And because the staff know their group of children well they can make more meaningful observations.

Tidy-up time

Tidy-up time involves more than just cleaning up the materials children have been working with. It enables children to learn not only where things go, and that similar things go together, thereby encouraging spatial and classification key experiences. Cleaning up at the end of work time helps children feel responsible for the materials they use and helps them to be aware of the effect they can make on the classroom environment.

Circle-time

Circle-time is when children and adults meet together as a whole group. During circle-time the group may sing and make up action songs, play musical instruments, move to music or play games. Circle-time may occur at the beginning of the session, as a transition activity, or at the conclusion of the session.

Outside-time

The High/Scope outdoor environment is planned to support children in vigorous physical activity, for example running, throwing, climbing. In addition it is resourced to enable the continuance of many curricular experiences which occur indoors, for example, painting, model making, sand and water play.

Snack-time

Snack-time provides not only for nutritional requirements, but is a time for developing skills and opportunities for experiencing different types of food.

Monitoring and assessment

Monitoring each child's development requires a system of regular *assessment*. The High/Scope programme encourages observation and regular recording of each child's activities using two record forms, Child Observation Records (COR) and Child Assessment Records (CAR). The CAR form is completed on a daily basis, whereas the COR form is a period summary of the CAR information. The CAR forms record the highest level of development in particular areas. On the basis of these, staff can judge what level the child has reached. For example, a child may indicate ability to classify objects by saying something like, 'That yellow circle looks like the moon.' Numerical ability could be monitored by recording instances such as, 'I want the red cubes because there are more.' Similarly, an understanding of the concept of time could be assessed by recording instances such as, 'My birthday is in the sunny time'; this is also indicative of the child's increasing capacity to relate past and future events. Such key experiences are noted by staff on the child's individual CAR form.

The CAR form can be used for daily planning: looking over the notes of several days can help staff plan for the next week. As staff review CAR forms when planning for each child, they may notice that some children have fewer entries in some areas than others, in other words some key experience areas are filled out less often or with less variety than others. This gap can be a signal to the planning team that extra attention should be paid to certain key experiences for a particular child. In this way a child's development can be supported.

The CAR form is short and simple – only statements describing children's actual behaviour are recorded. Entries on the CAR form are made at any time that is convenient for the staff. At first, the important thing is to get the information written down. Factual observations, such as 'he built a tower of twelve blocks' are much more useful than subjective statements, such as 'played nicely today with the blocks'. As staff gain more experience in filling in CAR forms, they find it easier to categorise events according to the key experiences and are more selective about entering only new information.

The COR form may be described as a summary of the CAR information. It may be administered at various points during the year. It measures developmental change over time and/or developmental status at a single point in time. Each COR form can be used up to three times per child. How the COR form is used depends upon the questions to be asked about the early years services and its participants. Staff may use COR forms during in-service sessions as a way of assessing the service and deciding which areas to strengthen or improve. The COR forms can also help staff members focus on the developmental abilities and needs of individual children.

Items on the form are organised into nine categories – using language, representing, classification, seriation, number concepts, spatial relations, temporal relations, movement, social and emotional – which correspond to the key experiences which we described at the beginning of the chapter, and which form the basis for the High/Scope curriculum. The key experiences are important in giving a focus to these observations and assessments and in identifying ways in which staff can support the child's development.

Table 3.1 shows how a member of staff can record a child's basic expressive vocabulary at one of four levels and at three points in time.

Table 3.1   Using language

	Basic expressive vocabulary	Time 1	2	3
(i)	Child only communicates in ways other than spoken language	1*	1	1
(ii)	Child uses a small number of words to communicate with adults and peers (eg: 'Lookit!' 'No!')	2	2	2
(iii)	Child's spoken language is adequate for communication	3	3	3
(iv)	Child's spoken vocabulary is large and varied	4	4	4

*1 represents the lowest level of attainment, 4 the highest. The adult circles the level 1–4 at each of the three time periods, on the basis of his or her observations of the child.

The CAR form enables direct recording of the child's progress in each of the areas that the High/Scope key experiences focus on. For example, language ability can be monitored by staff members recording children's utterances such as, 'I can't wear my new shoes outside because it is raining and they will get muddy and wet and dirty.' This kind of sentence would be noted by staff for its complexity; the child obviously has reasoned that he cannot wear his new shoes outside because the weather is too bad. On the COR form, for the basic expressive vocabulary section he or she would attain a score of (4). He or she is able to see the relationship between cause and effect. This sentence is more advanced than, 'I can't wear my shoes out', which shows no such complexity of thinking and would only attain a score of (3).

Room arrangement

Children's active learning and decision-making, and indeed the practicalities of operating High/Scope, are encouraged through a room arrangement where materials and equipment are accessible to the children, arranged in distinctive work areas, and 'labelled' in a way that they can understand. Once children have decided what to do they can find the necessary materials for their planned activity themselves and because everything belongs to a certain place, they can take responsibility for putting things back again. Work areas should be located around the perimeter of the room, with a central space for moving from one area to another and for group meetings and action games. The areas of the room that are considered the core areas of the High/Scope curriculum are the block area, the house area, the art area, the quiet area, and the outdoor play area. Adults may add other areas during the year as the children's interests become known to them.

Team teaching

Careful planning and staff discussion must take place if the High/Scope curriculum is going to work. Staff must decide what are the needs of both individual children and the group as a whole before they decide which aspects of the curriculum they should emphasise first. Obviously, staff consultation means that children are going to benefit from pooled opinions as opposed to one person's subjective opinion. The High/Scope curriculum calls this consultation and planning process 'team teaching'. It is a feature of the High/Scope classroom which is often not present in other classrooms. High/Scope regards all members of a team as having something important to contribute. Forty-five minutes to an hour every day with the whole team present and contributing is essential to the full implementation of the curriculum. The team can start off the planning process by selecting key experiences they feel are most appropriate for their children. They use the week's observations not only to guide their assessments of children but also to generate activities and teaching strategies. During this time, staff have the opportunity to discuss their personal feelings about a particular day. The analysis of such observations gives rise to useful and creative insights into a child's strengths and weakness. Perhaps it is here as much as anywhere that the role of the High/Scope trainer comes to the fore – in helping the whole staff group to share a common approach to their work. Through shared analysis of observation, staff can plan appropriate experiences that will guide each child to assume responsibility, take initiative, solve problems, make plans and be creative – thus achieving a balance of power and control.

Most important to the success of team teaching is what is known as the Programme Implementation Profile (PIP). This may be described as a type of manual that offers staff the opportunity to evaluate their own work, together with the training and support they have had and continue to receive. It is divided into sections, comprising questions which may be answered along a continuum. For example, aspects of the daily routine, adult–adult interaction, adult–child interaction, the physical environment may be assessed. There is a section on training which asks questions about how much training staff have received, whether they have meetings on a regular basis, as High/Scope recommends. This section is most important as it highlights how necessary it is to have support from managers with respect to in-service training. Also, including such a section helps to shift the evaluative focus on to the trainer as well as to staff; in this way staff can see that all aspects of the programme's use and implementation are being evaluated. The PIP also recognises the importance for staff to have time to evaluate and plan with each other. People often have the mistaken attitude that a pre-school educator's only task is to spend time with the children. The PIP can be seen as an assessment form to aid development in the adults whereas the COR and CAR forms are assessment tools used to support the development of the child.

Parental involvement

The early High/Scope programmes included involvement with parents through home visits, regular contact workshops and individual meetings. While home visits may not always be feasible (depending on staff resources and time constraints), parent involvement and the two-way flow of information (between carer and parent) are crucial. The early years service and its staff have knowledge and experience to offer to the family; the staff will also be informed and guided by the parents about the child, the family's culture, language and goals. The belief that parents and staff are both experts in their own domain is essential to the success of the programme and its use in a variety of settings, according to Weikart, the programme's principal evaluator.

High/Scope – the package

High/Scope can be viewed as a package, that is, it provides a cohesive framework: process and content are compatible and consistent and the practice ensuing will reflect the philosophy of the approach. Is it necessary to implement all the elements if one is to achieve a true High/Scope programme or can the 'package' be adapted to suit the needs of individual pre-schools or early years centres? This is an often-asked question. The answer it seems is that most pre-schools in the UK which are identified as High/Scope settings incorporate many of the elements of High/Scope. However, some of these settings may, for example, use key experiences as a focus for observation but then transfer this information to summative sheets required by their employing organisation instead of the COR and CAR forms, while others may not place as heavy an emphasis on setting time aside f   and planning with the whole team.

The High/Scope Institute who are the official body for all aspects pertaining to the High/Scope curriculum ... ...xam-ple running training courses, awarding accreditation to trainers and providing an information service – regard this as acceptable. They have come to see that High/Scope may be described better as a process, with more and more elements being incorporated over time. Although this flexible definition has its advantages, this may result in a degree of confusion as to what a High/Scope nursery actually is for anyone considering adopting the curriculum. A basic rule of thumb is that while it is not necessary to adopt all elements of the package in order to have a High/Scope nursery, there are some core elements which cannot be omitted; these are the plan/do/review element of the day, the emphasis on using key experiences to direct the child's learning and the role of the child as initiator and adult as facilitator and support. Underpinning the use of High/Scope will be an understanding of the philosophy of the approach and the role of the adult within it and reflecting it.

Comparing High/Scope with other pre-school curricula

In general, there are a recognised set of broad principles which underpin most pre-school curricula. High/Scope has much in common with the well-known Montessori schools, Schema-based curricula, the Playgroup movement, Froebel schools and the Irish-speaking Naíonraí. At the same time it has characteristics which set it apart. In many cases what really distinguishes a curricula are the specifics of the implementation – the way in which concepts are translated into practice and the particular emphasis that is given to individual elements. It is important to remember that there may well be a real gap between what people say their curriculum does and what actually happens in day-to-day practice.

Learning through play

Learning through play is a central component of many pre-school curricula. Indeed recognition of the value of this kind of learning is not a modern-day phenomena. Plato wrote that enforced learning will not stay in the mind and advised avoidance of compulsion (Pinder, 1987). Play, for Froebel, was a serious and deeply significant activity (Curtis, 1986). Kindergartens, for him, were institutions where children instruct and educate themselves, and where they develop and integrate all their abilities through play, which is creative activity and spontaneous instruction. However, he did ot believe that the play of young children should be unstructured, as was the approach of many of his later followers, and in order to help children learn through play he devised a series of playthings and games. According to Froebel, playing was the highest form of expression of the child's essence (Singer, 1992).

The philosophy behind the Playgroup Movement is one of learning through play, and emphasis is on the social benefits to young children of playing together without their parents. Their literature defines a playgroup as 'a group of 3–5 year old children exploring, discovering and adjusting socially through a play situation, under the guidance of responsible adults who are aware of the needs of pre-school children' (Statham, Lloyd and Moss, 1989). Similarly, the Naionrai groups (Irish-speaking pre-schools) emphasise the idea that children learn through play. However, Montessori's attitude to play and to imaginative play in particular is quite different and as such has been widely criticised (Curtis, 1986). She argued that the only form of play which was acceptable was that which had a preparatory function for adult forms of interaction. She considered fantasy play to be essentially dishonest, because in talking about stories involving witches and ogres or talking animals, children were being presented with a false picture of reality. High/Scope, on the other hand, recognises the value of play and much of the child's active learning, although it is termed the child's 'work', is in a structured play-type situation. Hence, the concept of learning through play is not new.

Learning and problem solving are active processes

Again, recognition of this is not a new phenomenon; Rousseau referred to the constant activity of the young, activity which enabled the child to acquire the concept of self. Montessori's attitude towards children was that they were active, intrinsically motivated beings, not passive learners who had to be 'force-fed' with information. The young child learned through observation, movement and exploration. Froebel believed that children learned best when engaged in creative activities springing from their own desires and educative experiences rather than a haphazard set of activities; hence it was imperative that they be presented with materials and ideas based on systematic planning. Similarly, High/Scope educators assume active learning to be central to the curriculum.

The autonomy of the child to make his or her own decisions

This also seems to be a central element of other curricula. Froebel,

Playgroup and Naíonraí curricula recognise the value of allowing children to make their own decisions. In the Montessori curriculum the freedom to choose work and to repeat an activity for any length of time are important factors in helping children to develop their personality and express their potential. However, in the Montessori class free-choice is not unconditional; it is more likely to mean that a child is given a choice of, say, three things which adults have presented, and allowed to choose one. Also, Montessori is also likely to assume that there is a set way of using materials – for example if the activity of the day is to allow children to dip their hands in paint and then make an imprint, then that is what a Montessori class will do, whereas a High/Scope class may have unrestricted access to the paints, without any prescribed instruction as to the appropriate or indeed only way to use them.

Daily routine

Having a daily routine is another consistent feature. Montessori believed that a planned environment was all important. In the Montessori pre-school children work individually most of the time, coming together when they wish to at different periods during a day. These periods arise out of the needs of the children on that particular day. A consistent routine provides a framework for all daily activity.

Room arrangement and materials

Central to the notion of a daily routine are *room arrangement* and appropriate *materials*. In the Montessori pre-school the rooms are arranged to convey as closely as possible a home for the children and not a school. Areas may be designed for quiet activities, reading, floor activities or table work. Where possible, free access to the garden is provided. The furniture is usually childsize. The shelves on which the materials and activities are displayed should be low enough for children to collect whatever they require with ease, whenever they require it. Children are free to choose the apparatus, which should be specific sense-training apparatus to be used in an exact manner within the classroom. Froebel worked out graduated exercises based on children's games, and designed simple educational apparatus, the 'gifts', to enable children to learn elementary laws of physical science and the eternal law of God. Froebel devised all sorts of 'occupations' such as folding paper, plaiting mats, making clay figures, sewing, embroidery and drawing. Songs, stories, conversations, movement games and gardening are other integral parts of the Froebel method. Providing a spacious, yet ordered room arrangement for young children which allows easy accessibility to developmentally appropriate toys and equipment, is a central feature of the High/Scope curriculum.

The teacher's role

The *teacher's role* seems quite similar whatever the specifics of the curriculum. For example, in the Montessori school the adult has four main tasks (Curtis, 1986). Firstly, it is to involve him or herself in a side by side learning situation with the child. Secondly, it is to provide a stimulating and challenging environment which will aid the child, by creating a spontaneous learning situation. Thirdly, it is to act as a link between the child and the materials. Fourthly, it is to observe each child, note what interests him or her, note how he or she works. He or she must also note how much freedom an individual child can cope with – and support his or her current needs. The teacher is the child's helper. He or she directs his or her exploration, as and when the child needs it. Similarly, the Playgroup movement fosters children's development under the guidance of responsible adults who are aware of the children's needs. The teacher's primary role in High/Scope is to facilitate and support the child's active learning. He or she silently observes, listens and enters into children's play using specific communication strategies which develop the child's problem solving abilities and frequently using a key experience as a focus for conversation.

The work of Athey (1990) and Nutbrown (1994) has highlighted the 'schema' concept present in many early years curricula. Basically a schema may be defined as 'a pattern of repeatable behaviour into which experiences are assimilated and that are gradually coordinated' (Athey, 1990, p.37). Teachers observe and extend activities which nourish children's schemas. For example, a simple extension of a child's vertical schema, might be allowing him or her to build a tower block with toy bricks. This could be compared to the way High/Scope teachers observe what and how children are doing throughout the daily routine via the key experiences and on the basis of these observations assess what the child can do and which key experiences should be encouraged. An important aspect of the High/Scope teacher's role is how he or she extends the child's thoughts and actions. For example, during work time he or she encourages the child to talk about what they are doing and may provide a narrative of what the child is actually doing.

Assessment and parental involvement

Regular *assessment* and *parental involvement* are other elements which are present to varying extents in most curricula. For example, planning and record keeping are important functions of the adult in the Montessori curriculum, just as in High/Scope. Parental involvement has always been integral to the Playgroup movement, with actual sessions sometimes (particularly in the past) being held in the homes of parents. So far, we have highlighted the elements that High/Scope shares with other curricula without reference to the important question that anyone interested in the High/Scope curriculum – potential 'consumers', academics, policy-makers – might ask: how is High/Scope different? In the following section, an attempt will be made to pinpoint the 'unique' features of High/Scope.

Is High/Scope different?

High/Scope is an approach which emphasises a balance of child and adult initiation. It places tremendous importance on the child as active learner. For active learning to be feasible in any pre-school environment, adjustments often have to be made. A pre-school where High/Scope is the curriculum of choice requires quite a distinctive room arrangement, with emphasis on well-defined work areas and most importantly giving the child the necessary physical space.

The plan/do/review element of the curriculum appears to be unique to High/Scope. Most importantly the plan/do/review sequence emphasises the child's responsibility for his or her own learning; the planning element makes the child think about what he or she wants to spend time doing – that is changing an impulse into a purpose; and the review element teaches the child to evaluate his or her actions which is a necessary component of efficient work. Other curricula may say that they encourage children to plan too; however, High/Scope actually formalises their plans and incorporates them into the daily routine. Indeed, Sylva (1994b) feels that High/Scope is unique in the way it enables language to be used to guide the action in work time and then to monitor and evaluate outcomes during the review session. Another element of the High/Scope curriculum which seems to distinguish it from other curricula is the particular emphasis on time set aside for staff feedback and planning. Having such time to examine observations and to plan what to do next is very important, and although not unique, is certainly unusual in the world of pre-school education.

The key experiences – the frameworks around which much of the work is organised – are specific to High/Scope. Furthermore,

High/Scope has a specific system of observation – the COR and CAR forms. Unlike a test that focuses on specific tasks performed outside the context of a child's regular activity, or a profile system that relies mostly on subjective assessment, the High/Scope Child Observation Record asks adults to record, in an objective, systematic way, the developmentally significant behaviours they observe in the daily activities of the children. Using the key experiences as the organising system, an accurate documentation of children's progress is achieved.

Finally, the level of choice that the curriculum allows the child and the striving towards real sharing of control seem to be particular features of High/Scope.

The advantages and disadvantages of High/Scope

For the child the fact that the adult acknowledges his or her ability to make sensible decisions is very important. High/Scope encourages children to be independent. As a result, very soon they try to solve things for themselves without first going to an adult. While some staff may find this hard to do, it is important, since giving children the opportunity to be problem-solvers enhances their self-esteem. Consistency is another important aspect; within High/Scope the rules are consistent, the daily routine is consistent, the room arrangement is consistent thus reflecting the philosophy. This means that the children are secure and hence gain the freedom to take risks and to try to do things for themselves.

For the adult, the curriculum helps him or her to see more clearly what children are interested in and what further experiences they would benefit from. The optimal situation is when children are interested in doing those things which encourage their development in all areas. From a practical point of view, High/Scope offers a curriculum in the widest sense of the word; a clear framework which can be introduced in a planned and consistent way into any early years setting.

In comparison to other 'looser' curricula, High/Scope might be accused of being too rigidly structured. Is there a danger that High/Scope-trained educators will unquestioningly follow the prescribed programme without thinking about what they are doing or why? A significant component of all High/Scope training courses is attention paid to reflecting upon the philosophy and principles of the approach. If people are given guidelines but allowed a certain amount of autonomy and flexibility in how they adhere to them, they actually produce something fresh and innovative, a fact which High/Scope is increasingly recognising. However, it would seem that High/Scope is less likely to allow this to happen creatively and spontaneously; by the same token the very consistency of the High/Scope approach does mean that if followed correctly High/Scope helps to ensure acceptable high standards of pre-school education.

The introduction of High/Scope to Britain and Ireland

Although High/Scope has played an important role in the world of pre-school education in the United States of America for almost 30 years, interest in Britain and Ireland has been fairly recent. The first course of training for High/Scope trainers in the UK took place in 1984, with a second two years later. Since then there has been a consistent uptake of training courses, resulting in the introduction of the curriculum. By March 1995 there were ninety endorsed trainers in Britain. There has been little evaluation of the training courses, although the early ones which were funded by the Aga Khan Foundation, the Gulbenkian Foundation and an anonymous donor, and coordinated by VOLCUF (Voluntary Organisations Liaison Council for Under-Fives) were evaluated by a team of researchers from Oxford University led by Kathy Sylva. The report by these evaluators pointed to the variable success in implementation but with more positives than negatives. While some trainers dropped out, the outcomes for others depended on their level of commitment, their role and status within their organisation and the commitment of their managers. Moreover, of the ten organisations who financed trainers, eight were intending to continue and develop their use of High/Scope (Sylva, Smith and Moore, 1986; Moore and Smith, 1987). One year after taking up High/Scope, these staff reported changes in the children in terms of 'active-learning', self-determination, independence, decision-making for themselves, self-expression, problem solving, as well as particular improvements in children's speech, language development, concentration span and reduction in disruptive behaviour.

The introduction of a new curriculum cannot be achieved quickly, but rather requires several stages. Weikart used an analogy to describe these stages to Sylva and colleagues. He felt that when anyone first learns a new set of principles there is a tendency to 'cook book' them or apply them somewhat rigidly. It is only as staff gain confidence and experience that they become more sure of their ability to take educational advantage of the situations which arise, they feel less need to control things and can move from a 'structured' to an 'open framework'. (Sylva, Smith and Moore,

1986). This was indeed reflected in the experiences of the first trainers, who reported a continuous process of thinking, experimenting, and adapting to suit the particular needs of each centre.

The introduction of High/Scope to Barnardo's

Barnardo's in the UK were heavily involved in providing day care for children 'at risk' and children experiencing considerable social disadvantage. While they aimed to offer a high-quality service, the approach taken was one of care rather than education, and given the 'at risk' status of most of the children, this seemed quite appropriate. However, Barnardo's also recognised the need to ensure that their day care was both structured and focused and hence began to rethink curriculum development within their day centres. Three criteria were identified as necessary for any curriculum:

- it must provide a purposeful programme that is appropriate to disadvantaged children and their families. In particular it should equip the children to cope better with the demands of school, and should encourage the parents and reduce their sense of hopelessness through the achievements of their children;
- it should be a culturally sensitive approach that can help children from different ethnic backgrounds;
- the training programme should be interdisciplinary and appropriate to all levels of staff.

Barnardo's felt that High/Scope had the potential to meet these criteria. The positive experiences of those on the early training course encouraged Barnardo's to maintain a strong interest in High/Scope in terms of supporting trainers, equipping centres and through financial input into High/Scope UK.

Barnardo's in Ireland became interested in 1979 when the then director attended a seminar at which the research outcomes, including the 'sleeper effects' of the Headstart Programme, were outlined. During the mid-1980s, as part of their continuing appraisal of services, Barnardo's was seeking a suitable curriculum for its under-fives units. The then Project Leader in Tallaght attended a seminar conducted by Dr David Weikart, President of the High/Scope Foundation, in Dublin in 1983 and subsequently visited the High/Scope Centre in Ypsilanti, Michigan, to observe the programme more closely. In 1986, it was decided to appoint a full time High/Scope Trainer who would work in Millbrook Nursery.

The three criteria listed earlier by which Barnardo's judged the suitability of a curriculum were felt to be equally applicable in Ireland. The more specific elements that provided impetus for the adoption of the High/Scope curriculum by Barnardo's in the Republic of Ireland have been identified and are listed below:

- It was hoped that High/Scope would complement the existing care-oriented approach. Furthermore, High/Scope was not philosophically in conflict with the other approaches to pre-school education in Ireland, including Montessori or NNEB Certificate in Child Care courses. It was hoped that it would provide a consistency of approach for the training of pre-school workers currently working within the service. Having an over-all structure and modus operandi which would give staff a common programme or curriculum, and a strong basis for teamwork, was convincingly attractive. Up to that time, the day care units had experienced a mixture of staff disciplines and training procedures. Adopting one specific curriculum which would be in keeping with the philosophy of the nursery, could only enhance the quality of pre-school care and education available. This was one of the primary reasons for Barnardo's interest in High/Scope.

- It was hoped to harness the already excellent standards of care into a programme that would more consciously use cognitive and other intellectually stimulating components and hence do even more for these disadvantaged children by giving them solid tools with which to approach formal education in primary school.

- In terms of the specific educational needs of these children, it was felt that the plan/do/review aspect of the High/Scope curriculum would be particularly useful. Such a structure is particularly important to the child from a disadvantaged home where there may be little structure and daily routine. Similarly, the plan/do/review sequence provides inbuilt limits for the teacher, in that there are certain parts of the routine of which the children must retain ownership.

- A new curriculum emphasising parent–child interaction and parent involvement could have a stronger impact on the home environment, thereby capitalising on the child's enhanced experience at the day care centre. High/Scope seemed to offer these elements.

- Senior members were particularly interested in (a) a pre-school programme that could be systematically assessed and (b) the potential for follow-up once children had entered primary school. The system of day care up until 1987 had focused more on care than education. As a result, there was no emphasis on collecting outcome data, and pertinent and valuable feedback regarding the children's progress was not available. High/Scope could alter this in terms of providing an educational focus and offering a credible benchmark by which to follow-up progress in schools.

- Barnardo's needed to be known not only as a professional body, but also as a body whose services – especially in day care – were filling an urgent need. In order to raise appropriate funding for those services from the relevant Government bodies it was necessary to demonstrate positive outcomes. It was felt that this need could be partially met by publicity in relation to High/Scope. This would not be the main aim of implementing High/Scope, but would be a very valuable and valid offshoot.

On a practical note, by early 1987 Barnardo's in the UK had already invested a significant amount of resources in introducing and developing High/Scope in the UK and in transferring skills and training from the USA, so were particularly interested in seeing how it would work in their facilities in Ireland.

Conclusion

High/Scope shares many of the elements of other good-quality preschool curricula; however the way in which these elements are combined or emphasised does make High/Scope different. Some aspects of the curriculum, for example the plan/do/review element of the daily routine and the use of the key experiences to guide children's active learning seem to be specific to High/Scope.

Although High/Scope has been in use in the USA for over thirty years now, interest in Britain and Ireland is fairly recent. In fact, this present research is the first evaluation, to date, of a nursery using High/Scope in Ireland or indeed in Britain. The following two chapters introduce the specifics of this research project – the subjects, type of assessments carried out, methodology, research site – and an account of the day-to-day, on-site operation of High/Scope.

Appendix

High/Scope Pre-school Key Experiences

Creative representation

- Recognising objects by sight, sound, touch, taste and smell
- Imitating actions and sounds
- Relating models, pictures, and photographs to real places and things
- Pretending and role-playing
- Making models out of clay, blocks, and other materials
- Drawing and painting

Language and literacy

- Talking with others about personally meaningful experiences
- Describing objects, events, and relations
- Having fun with language: listening to stories and poems, making up stories and rhymes
- Writing in various ways: drawing, scribbling, letterlike forms, invented spelling, conventional forms
- Reading in various ways: reading storybooks, signs, symbols, one's own writing
- Dictating stories

Initiative and social relations

- Making and expressing choices, plans and decisions
- Solving problems encountered in play
- Taking care of one's own needs
- Expressing feelings in words
- Participating in group routines
- Being sensitive to the feelings, interests and needs of others

- Building relationships with children and adults
- Creating and experiencing collaborative play
- Dealing with social conflict

Classification

- Exploring and describing similarities, differences and the attributes of things
- Distinguishing and describing shapes
- Sorting and matching
- Using and describing something in several ways
- Holding more than one attribute in mind at a time
- Distinguishing between 'some' and 'all'
- Describing characteristics something does not posseSs or what class it does not belong to

Seriation

- Comparing attributes (longer/shorter, bigger/smaller)
- Arranging several things one after another in a series or pattern and describing the relationships (big/bigger/biggest, red/blue/red/blue)
- Fitting one ordered set of objects to another through trial and error (small cup–small saucer/medium cup–medium saucer/big cup–big saucer)

determine 'more', 'fewer', 'same amount'

- Arranging two sets of objects in one-to-one correspondence
- Counting objects

Movement

- Moving in non-locomotor ways (anchored movement: bending, twisting, rocking, swinging one's arms)
- Moving in locomotor ways (non-anchored movement: running, jumping, hopping, skipping, marching, climbing)
- Moving with objects
- Expressing creativity in movement
- Describing movement
- Acting upon movement directions
- Moving in sequences to a common beat

Music

- Moving to music
- Exploring and identifying sounds
- Exploring one's singing voice
- Developing melody
- Singing songs
- Playing simple instruments

Space

- Filling and emptying
- Fitting things together and taking them apart
- Changing the shape and arrangement of objects (wrapping, twisting, stretching, stacking, enclosing)
- Observing, people, things and places from different spatial viewpoints
- Experiencing and describing positions, directions, and distances in the play space, building and neighbourhood
- Interpreting spatial relations in drawings, pictures and photographs

Time

- Starting and stopping an action on signal
- Experiencing and describing rates of movement
- Experiencing and comparing time intervals
- Anticipating, remembering and describing sequences of events

4. The research study

In the early chapters we discussed the context in which this research study has been located; setting out the evidence on the effectiveness of early years pre-schooling, presenting a broad picture of pre-school and school services in Ireland, noting in particular the context of social disadvantage, and then looking in some detail at the High/Scope curriculum. We turn now to the particulars of the research study.

Barnardo's is a child care charity which has been running services in Ireland since the 1960s. One of its pre-schools, located in a particularly disadvantaged area of Dublin, adopted the High/Scope curriculum in the mid-1980s. By the early 1990s, Barnardo's were eager to evaluate the process and commissioned the National Children's Bureau to undertake an independent research study. This chapter outlines that research project. First, the research goals are established. An account is given of the research site – the area in which the pre-school is located, and the type of difficulties experienced by the sample group. The subject groups, the measures used, the methodology – how and where the data was collected over a time period of three years – are described in detail.

Research site

Tallaght

The subject of this study, Millbrook Nursery, is situated in the West Dublin suburb of Tallaght. Tallaght was constructed at a time of increasing urbanisation and unprecedented population growth in the Greater Dublin area. It was hoped that this new town would contribute substantially towards meeting the social and economic needs of the large and predominantly young population which located there. However, Tallaght was designed and implemented without the benefit of a local development agency.

Instead, there was a division of responsibility between existing state agencies and statutory bodies whose administrative boundaries did not always coincide. It is the country's fourth largest urban centre, yet it remains without such basic necessities as a hospital.

Provision of housing

Between 1971 and 1981 the number of houses in the area increased from 1,352 to just under 18,000. In addition to those on the housing list (mainly young families), the populations of some older, declining inner city communities were relocated to Tallaght. More recent development, predominantly in the public sector, has occurred in the more outlying and more physically and socially isolated areas to the west (these are the areas where most of this study's subjects live), while private sector housing tends to be predominantly in the east. As a result the east/west distinction within the area has become more visible in recent years, with large-scale concentration of disadvantage in certain areas of West Tallaght in particular. Research carried out by Jobstown Integrated Development Project and West Tallaght Resource Centre (cited in The Community Development Projects of the Tallaght Partnership) has identified a number of specific problems relating to housing; these include poor maintenance, lack of adequate warmth, lack of involvement of residents in the decisions made about their estates, growing waiting-lists associated with the general housing shortage in Dublin, problems created by inappropriate local government boundaries and the absence of an adequate environmental plan for Tallaght.

Table 4.1   Age structure for Tallaght and Ireland

Age group	Tallaght	Republic of Ireland
0–14	39%	27%
15–24	18%	17%
25–44	31%	27%
45–64	11%	18%
65+	.01%	11%
Total	62,785	3,525,719

Source: Census 1991 data.

Social mix

While overall there are fewer professional workers and more manual workers in Tallaght than in either Dublin city or county, within the area there is wide variation. In July 1990 the proportion of the workforce engaged in professional occupations stood at less than five per cent in West Tallaght.

The demographic profile

As a result of the rapid expansion of Tallaght since 1971, and the predominance of young families among the population, there are now quite distinct and unique population patterns within the area. In 1991 there were approximately 62,785[1] people living in Tallaght, of which 31,156 were male and 31,629 were female. Table 4.1 illustrates the population breakdown by age in Tallaght, as compared to figures for the whole population of Ireland (Census 1991 data). We can see from this the very high proportion of the population who are aged 0 to 14 years. This proportion is higher in Tallaght than for the country as a whole; correspondingly the figure for the 45 years plus age-group was 29 per cent for the country as a whole, and 11 per cent in Tallaght.

Table 4.2   Classification by sex

Age group	% Male	% Female
0–14	52	48
15–24	51	49
25–44	46	54
45–64	52	48
65+	38	62

Marital status

Census 1991 data revealed that 61 per cent of males were single, 38 per cent are/had been married, and less than 1 per cent were widowed. Of the females 57 per cent were single, 41 per cent were/had been married and only a very small number were widowed.

---

1   The total population figure of 62,785 people was obtained by summing the numbers of people living in the 13 electoral divisions classified by the 1991 Census as belonging to Tallaght – Avonbeg, Belgard, Fettercairn, Glenview, Jobstown, Killinarden, Kilnamanagh, Kiltipper, Kingswood, Millbrook, Oldbawn, Springfield, Tymon.

Unemployment/employment

The decline in manufacturing industry and in the public and private services sectors has meant that neither the local nor the wider labour markets have been able to cater for the employment needs of Tallaght, and in the 1990s the unemployment rate is higher than for the rest of the country – 24 per cent compared with the national average of 21.8 per cent. In November 1993, there were 7,049 people in receipt of social welfare payments, two-thirds of whom were male and one-third female. Over one-third were long-term unemployed, that is without a job for at least 15 months. Within Tallaght, the highest levels of unemployment are in the west, that part of Tallaght in which Millbrook Nursery is located.

Women in Tallaght

Women are particularly disadvantaged in a variety of ways. They lose out in a whole range of areas such as education, public and private employment, training, the law and the benefits system. Lack of adequate child care facilities is an important barrier to taking up training, education and employment opportunities. Over 30 per cent of women in Tallaght who are unemployed are long-term unemployed, compared with a national average of 25 per cent. Of those who are employed, many are in low-paid and part-time jobs with little security or enforceable rights.

Education

The relationship between education and poverty has already been highlighted in Chapter 2. Many studies show that social class influences access to and participation in education in terms of duration (Whelan and Whelan, 1984), sector attended (Clancy, 1982), curriculum provided (Breen, 1986) and transfer rates to third-level studies (Clancy, 1982, 1988). Overall, studies show that children from manual backgrounds, and particularly those from unskilled and semi-skilled backgrounds, are less likely than their counterparts from other social backgrounds to complete the post-primary junior cycle, to make the transition from junior to senior cycle, or to transfer to higher or third-level education. Among the adult population of Tallaght, there is evidence of considerably lower rates of participation in education and earlier school-leaving than is the case nationally (Ronayne and Duggan, 1990). All this indicates that the children in this study are likely to experience difficulties regarding entry to the labour market.

Primary education

There are 3,223 national schools in Ireland. Of these, 258 (eight per cent) are designated 'disadvantaged'. Disadvantaged schools are schools which the Department of Education recognises as containing a large number of pupils from socially deprived backgrounds. Such schools are allocated additional staffing and resources. There are 34 national schools in Tallaght; of these 15 (44 per cent) fit this disadvantaged category. Fifteen schools in total participated in this study. Of these, 14 were located in Tallaght and eight (57 per cent) belonged to the disadvantaged category.

Health facilities and services

The Eastern Health Board (EHB) is responsible for the provision of health care facilities in the area. Since there are as yet no hospital facilities, health services are provided mainly through health centres at three locations within Tallaght. These centres provide children's health clinics, speech therapy, psychiatric clinics, public health nursing, drugs counselling and advice directed towards deprived families. There are also services provided by the EHB in conjunction with voluntary agencies, such as Barnardo's, including special classes for Traveller children, community nursing services, day centres for the elderly and child guidance centres. There remains, however, a shortfall between the services that are provided and the requirements of the local population.

Positive developments

In Tallaght, local groups and organisations have begun to work in partnership with government departments and state agencies in identifying areas of local need, delivering services and providing facilities. A wide range of local groups and organisations have emerged. Many of these provide opportunities in the areas of sport, culture and the arts and are primarily concerned with improving the quality of life generally. In addition, there are local groups and organisations that address more specifically the economic and social circumstances of the local population and, either solely or more usually in conjunction with one or more statutory agencies, provide services in the area of education, health advice and support, welfare information and personal development. The Jobstown Integrated Development Project is working on the development of family support services such as pre-school, and mother and toddler groups. Indeed, local action in Tallaght has made a considerable contribution to the well-being of the local population. Tallaght Welfare Society, for example, receives 35,000 requests for information each year and provides over 200 individuals and families with a Home Help service.

Millbrook Nursery

The Millbrook Nursery forms part of the Tallaght Family Services Project. This project, which is operated by Barnardo's, provides services for young children and their families, with the focus on enabling them to cope as a family in the community. Maximum participation and involvement from all parents is encouraged. The Millbrook Nursery is only one branch of the entire project. Other services include parent education groups, after-schools groups and a toy library service.

The provision of day care services and a sessional group facility in Millbrook Nursery provides a much-needed support for families in periods of crisis or stress. Parent groups emphasise parenting skills but also recognise parents as individuals with their own needs. The toy library and Family Advisory services reach the families of children with 'special needs'. The primary aim of the toy library service is to help parents to realise the potential that their child possesses and to take pride in their child's achievements. Parental and community involvement are essential ingredients in the functioning of the toy library. The methods employed by the toy library worker are designed to encourage self-sufficiency in both parents and children, mainly enabling the parent to understand the exact nature of the child's needs. This service allows children to exchange toys on a weekly or fortnightly basis, in this way increasing their opportunities for exploration and creative play. It provides opportunity for social contact for children who do not attend playgroups. Nursery staff act in an advisory capacity to parents and incorporate a general monitoring of the family situation as part of their work programme, reporting to the Eastern Health Board and Community Care Social Worker.

In 1987, Barnardo's decided to incorporate the High/Scope curriculum within its existing service at the Millbrook Nursery. Barnardo's were keen to evaluate this process through an independent research study, so in 1991 the National Children's Bureau were commissioned to undertake a three-year research study.

Research goals

This study had four key research goals. These were to provide:

(i) an insight into the operation of High/Scope at the Millbrook Nursery as perceived by staff and parents;

(ii) an indication of how well-prepared nursery 'graduates' were for starting primary school;

(iii) an overview of the children's progress in primary school, one and two years after leaving the nursery;

(iv) an indication of how these children were functioning – cognitively, emotionally and socially – as compared to peers who had not graduated from Millbrook.

While this study was not an attempt to replicate the American Perry Project referred to in Chapter 1, it was obviously influenced by it.

Research methods

To meet the research goals, a research study was designed with data collection taking place in two rounds. Round one took place at the nursery throughout late 1991 and early 1992; round two took place in schools over the two school years 1992–3 and 1993–4. During round one, in-depth interviews were conducted with both nursery staff and the High/Scope Trainer to explore staff opinions regarding the implementation of High/Scope and to help ascertain the children's progress. Interviews with parents were conducted at the nursery and provided additional information about some of the children. An account of these interviews will be presented in the following chapters. Educational and psychological testing of the children who had attended Millbrook took place over a period of three years and of the contrast group for a period of two years. Assessments carried out in the pre-school are referred to as round one data. The assessments which took place towards the end of the children's first and second years of schooling are referred to as round two /first stage and round two /second stage respectively.

Round one

The focus of round one was an evaluation of the use of High/Scope at the day nursery. This involved an investigation of the introduction and implementation process of High/Scope at the nursery, and secondly, the development of individual profiles of all the children in the sample group, according to their performance on a variety of psychometric measures.

The sample

In the first year, the sample consisted of all 22 children at the nursery who would be of an age to attend primary school in September 1992. Ages ranged from three years to four years six months when they entered Millbrook Nursery in September 1991. All these children came from very poor socio-economic backgrounds. Moreover, in many cases families would have been regarded as dysfunctional by child care and child welfare professionals who had made the initial referrals to the nursery. An account of the initial referral circumstances surrounding each of these children, with particular emphasis on their home backgrounds, is presented in Appendix C. Children were initially presenting with behaviour problems; these were viewed more as a manifestation of their home circumstances than as inbuilt characteristics. These problems are discussed in more detail later in this chapter.

Measures

Data was gathered using a range of standardised tests, together with other methods, including observation and interview. A variety of tests were administered to the children:

- British Ability Scales;
- Goodenough-Harris Draw-A-Man Test;
- Vineland Adaptive Behaviour Scale;
- Reynell Developmental Language Scales (Second Revision).

As well as these specific measures, information was gathered from other sources:

- Behavioural Screening Questionnaire;
- Child Observation Record (COR) forms;
- Video recordings;
- Parent interviews;
- Staff interviews.

Data collection procedure

Children were tested on two short cognitive measures (the British Ability Scales took approximately 20 minutes to complete and the Goodenough-Harris Draw-A-Man Test between ten and 15 minutes) and on a measure of language ability (Reynell Developmental Language Scales) towards the end of the year. Nursery staff completed COR forms usually midway through and at the end of the year, and the behavioural measures (Behaviour Screening Questionnaire (BSQ), Vineland Adaptive Behaviour Scales) were administered towards the end of the year. While the BSQ could be completed quickly, the Vineland Adaptive Behaviour Scales required more detailed attention and were more time-consuming. A detailed description of all psychometric tests used is presented in Appendix A. Video recordings of day-to-day functioning of the groups were made midway through and at the end of the year, with a view to monitoring any qualitative changes in the children's functioning. These also provided a useful means of feedback to staff and were a means for generating information from staff on an informal level and for building up initial rapport with the children. Lengthy interviews were conducted with staff at different points throughout the year by the researchers. Parent interviews were conducted in order to gauge their reactions to the work conducted at the nursery and to elicit views concerning the children's progress.

Round two/first stage

In round two the focus moved to the primary schools. The research examined the transition to school of the High/Scope children and followed them up towards the end of their first year there. Comparison was made with a similar group of children who had not experienced High/Scope.

The sample

For round two, the sample consisted of two groups – Group A and Group B. Group A consisted of 21 of the children from round one who had attended the Millbrook Nursery in Tallaght and were now attending local primary schools. Group B consisted of a contrast group of 20 children. Both groups of children were matched in terms of socio-economic circumstances and where they lived. It was felt by welfare professionals that both groups would have benefited from attending the nursery and all had been referred to the nursery. However, Group B children were further down the waiting list, primarily because they were not experiencing the same extent of family disruption or dysfunction as Group A children. Hence, Group B children did not get places at the nursery. The main contrast between the two groups was that unlike Group A, Group B children had not attended Millbrook Nursery nor received the High/Scope curriculum (although most had some kind of pre-school experience).

Measures

The following standardised tests were used with both groups of children in their first year at school (again, these are described in detail in Appendix A):

- British Ability Scales (BAS);
- Vineland Adaptive Behaviour Scales;

- Preschool Behaviour Checklist;
- Perceived Competence and Social Acceptance Scales (PCSA).

Data collection procedure

Each child from both groups was individually assessed by the author at his or her school. Cognitive testing took place first. All the children in a particular school (in most cases no more than three children) were tested on the cognitive measure prior to testing on the self-esteem measure. Hence, each child had a break between the two testing sessions. For example, he or she might have completed the cognitive test (BAS) in the morning and the self-esteem measure (PCSA) in the afternoon. The self-esteem measure usually took no longer than 15 to 20 minutes. Before the children were assessed, teachers were given a behavioural checklist (the Preschool Behaviour Checklist) to complete for each child, and requested to do so usually before the end of the school day. This took between eight to ten minutes to complete. Teachers were also interviewed by the author about the children's social/emotional behaviour and asked to complete the teacher section of the self-esteem measure (this took no more than five minutes approximately) once testing had been completed.

Round two/second stage

Data collection for the second stage of round two took place a year after round one. The children were assessed on each of the measures mentioned below during their second year of primary schooling.

The sample

Of the 41 children, only one child in Group A could not be traced in the follow-up. Both groups now consisted of 20 children, and these became the sample for subsequent analyses of data.

Measures

The tests used in this final stage are listed below (and detailed in Appendix A).

- British Ability Scales;
- Perceived Competence and Social Acceptance Scales;
- Prosocial Behaviour Questionnaire;
- Child Behaviour Questionnaire.

Data collection procedure

Testing was conducted in exactly the same manner as in the previous year. None of the children had been retained in class, all had moved from junior to senior infants level. Teachers were given checklists (usually at the beginning of the day) and asked to complete them as soon as possible.

Research subjects

Many of the Group A children had been referred to the nursery as a result of difficulties in areas that the High/Scope curriculum claims to address: particularly – cognitive/academic, language and social/emotional functioning. Of the 22 children from Group A, seven had been in attendance at the nursery for two years. A full account of the initial referral circumstances of each of the children is presented in Appendix C. To illustrate some of these circumstances here, we report the observations of the staff on the children's response to attending the nursery.

With regard to general cognitive and language functioning, limited concentration span and lack of expressive speech were difficulties often mentioned by the nursery supervisor: 'He was referred by the public health nurse because she felt he was quite delayed and had very little speech.' Another child had been assessed as mildly mentally handicapped and there was a query as to whether some of the others should attend a special school as opposed to an ordinary primary school: 'I think he would have been a candidate for St Joseph's (special school) without some intervention' (nursery supervisor). Encouragingly, staff noted visible improvements in many children by the end of the year: 'He became quite articulate and together, and chatted with the other children. Overall, I think he did really well.'

Concerns also surrounded the children's social/emotional functioning. Difficulty in relating to other children was a common problem. One child in particular was experiencing trouble in separating from his mother, and in mixing with other adults and children: 'The whole separation thing was a nightmare for him, with the result that he presented with some strange behaviour, in the way that he wouldn't make eye contact with people, his whole body posture was very shy and withdrawing.' Difficulties in settling in initially, and in cooperating with other children and sharing were mentioned: 'His level of cooperation with other children was very limited – he found it difficult to take direction from anyone even within the family.' Some children were particularly shy and withdrawn at first: 'She tended to talk only to her younger sister, she was extremely stubborn and would just go into total silence. You couldn't get her to communicate with you at all', and 'He was shy with other children, found it difficult to mix and quite shy with other adults as well.' In some cases children were fearful at first: 'He was very fretful...he was afraid to move out even, and try new material that might be presented to him. Everything terrified him.' Basic skills such as toilet-training had not been acquired by some children. Another child had been referred to the nursery because of queries over non-accidental injury; social workers were particularly worried about bruising. This child's attention-seeking and demanding behaviour created problems in the nursery at the beginning of the year.

Group B children came from the same geographic area and experienced the same level of economic deprivation as Group A children. Their circumstances also rendered them eligible for a place in the nursery. Staff identified a range of possible reasons why they were not successful at gaining places; for example they may not have been as well-known to the selection committee (comprised of Barnardo's staff, a medical representative and a social worker), or the families did not present in time for a place at the nursery. In some cases, the level of social disadvantage and familial disruption may not have been as extreme as for Group A children. Typical difficulties included language deficits and inability to relate well to each other. Some children were disruptive or generally anxious, or were delayed in attaining developmental milestones.

Group B children had all had some kind of pre-schooling experience. For example, six children had attended a toy library service. Others attended community-based playgroups. Barnardo's have had input in the setting up of many of these groups, and indeed often continue to work with them through their advisory service, offering support, advice, information and training. However, assessing the quality of the varied pre-school experience of Group B children was just not feasible in the way that it was for the High/Scope group. We must remember that toy libraries are limited in their educational focus, and do not require children to separate from their parents. Community playgroups usually have sessions of two to two-and-a-half hours duration, four days a week. A typical session may begin with free play, with children choosing from a variety of activities such as painting or jigsaws. There is usually a short break for refreshments, which is often followed by group-time (group activities such as singing). Hence, some elements are reminiscent of High/Scope, but there is no way of assessing to what degree high standards are maintained.

Conclusion

In conclusion, we can see that the design of the present study is loosely based on the original Perry Preschool Project research. The research site – Tallaght – is a disadvantaged area of Dublin and hence shares some of the characteristics particular to the area in Ypsilanti, Michigan, in which the Perry sample group lived. Overall goals are similar, sample groups are alike. However, the Perry control group had no pre-school experience whereas the contrast group in this study had some contact with various early years services. Also, while the Perry research has been ongoing over the last three decades, the present study is a much shorter-term evaluation over a period of three years. In the following chapter we will retrace our steps and explore why and how High/Scope was adopted and implemented in the nursery, in particular why High/Scope was felt to be appropriate for children from an area such as Tallaght, and what this meant in terms of staff training and reorganising an existing nursery into a High/Scope environment.

5. High/Scope in action

The aim of this chapter is to show the reader how the High/Scope curriculum (described in detail in Chapter 3) could be adopted and successfully implemented in a pre-school which had previously had a less formal and uniform curriculum. The type of training staff received to complement their own professional backgrounds, the obvious changes necessitated by the introduction of this curriculum, the way children adapted and reacted to various aspects of High/Scope, together with the type of cases that presented at the nursery, will be outlined in detail.

Training staff to use High/Scope

The training process

The first practical step taken by Barnardo's with regard to introducing the curriculum to the nursery in general, and to existing staff in particular, was to appoint a staff member who would subsequently be trained as a High/Scope Trainer at the High/Scope Institute in London. Once recruited, training commenced in September 1987 with the first two-week block of the 'Training of Trainers UK Wave II' course. This session was followed by five one-week blocks in November 1987, January, March, April and May 1988. The Trainer received her High/Scope endorsement in March 1989. A requirement of the training was to actively train staff while implementing the High/Scope programme.

Work at Millbrook Nursery commenced with a pilot group involving one full-time pre-school worker, one part-time pre-school worker and one team worker. High/Scope training sessions for nursery staff were held once a month. Furthermore, the Trainer continued to work at non-participant observations followed by weekly individual feedback sessions with all the staff. By September 1988, all nursery staff were involved. Trainer and Supervisor met weekly, while both met with the Project Leader on a monthly basis. The Trainer had three-weekly support sessions with the Project Leader and they in turn liaised with senior Barnardo's staff from both the UK and Ireland. Support and validation of staff members' previous training were reported as the most important aspects of training sessions. The Nursery Supervisor felt that there was more of a 'team' approach to working with the children once High/Scope was introduced. The fact that the Trainer was on site and readily available to staff was very important during the early stages of the High/Scope implementation process (and indeed was unusual). This ensured that queries and problems could be discussed on the spot and the appropriate action taken, and that the High/Scope curriculum was implemented in an organised and coherent manner such that the quality of the overall programme was maintained.

Staff background and experience

The person appointed to the post of High/Scope Trainer was qualified as a social worker. While she had much experience of working with young children, her particular area of expertise was in behaviour modification. The post required her to work closely with and be accountable to the Project Leader.

The Project Leader for the Tallaght Family Services Project was involved in the coordination and organisation of a range of services including: the provision of early education and sessional group facility at Millbrook Nursery (involving the use of the High/Scope curriculum); the provision of groups which facilitate and encourage child/parent interaction; provision of a toy library and family advisory service; parent support groups; and an outreach service in West Tallaght to extend and support the work of the project. Her own theoretical and training background consisted of a Higher Diploma in Education, Diploma in Montessori Education, High/Scope training, Diploma in Supervision and First Line Management. Her primary experience had been in teaching, pre-school education, working with Travellers and managing the Tallaght team.

At the beginning of the High/Scope implementation process, the Nursery Supervisor was on a two-day release to attend lectures as part of a national pre-school training programme. By September 1989 she had completed this course and returned to the nursery full-time. The responsibility for supporting existing, and initiating new, staff then shifted from the Trainer to the Nursery Supervisor. The nursery staff came to High/Scope from a variety of professional backgrounds. One had a degree in psychology, two had qualifications in Montessori teaching, one had qualifications in pre-school education and social studies, another a qualification in pre-school education and a child care qualification in mental handicap. Depending on their training backgrounds, some staff found it easier to adapt to the High/Scope method than others. According to the Nursery Supervisor, staff who had been Montessori-trained seemed to experience most difficulties in changing to the High/Scope approach. Staff who had completed the National Certificate in Early Childhood Care and Education, run by the Dublin Institute of Technology, adapted well to using High/Scope, possibly because different early education approaches including High/Scope had been explored in their training.

In contrast to the staff in the nursery, staff in most of the other early years facilities attended by the study's contrast group would have had little or no formal pre-school training. Some of those who ran community playgroups had completed the IPPA (Irish Pre-school Playgroups Association) foundation courses; toy library supervisors may have been qualified in other areas – for example one supervisor was a registered nurse – but toy libraries were staffed, in the main, by volunteers.

Getting High/Scope up and running

When staff are straight out of college, or have worked in a certain way for years, they tend to find the changes the High/Scope curriculum requires demanding. The 'room arrangement' is a structural change, and is not generally a difficult transition for staff to make. Recording their observations and giving and receiving feedback at daily team meetings is more difficult. However, not teaching in a directive way is probably the hardest thing for staff to get used to. Indeed, the High/Scope Trainer described the most difficult aspects of the changeover to High/Scope as: 'Staff "letting go" of some of the control and becoming more aware of how they talked to children. Also a more structured routine and emphasis on planning for the staff.'

The plan/do/review sequence is a feature unique to High/Scope. The review aspect of the plan/do/review is more difficult to get right than the planning part. Small-group time can also be quite difficult to adjust to. This is adult-initiated, but also supposed to give the child choice. It is unusual to adopt all elements of the High/Scope package at once. In the next section, we report how staff gradually changed their environment and methods of working as they adapted to the High/Scope curriculum.

The physical environment

The introduction of High/Scope resulted in a variety of physical changes to the existing arrangements. High shelving and a sunken tiled area presented safety hazards to the children. As the Project Leader pointed out, constantly trying to redirect the children and worrying about the physical threat to them in relation to this area threatened the optimal implementation of the High/Scope programme. Until the shelving was lowered, the High/Scope principle that the room should be laid out in such a way that the children could see all the material at a glance could not be adhered to. Hence, appropriate changes to the safety features of the room and to the shelving played a significant part in introducing the High/Scope curriculum.

The room was divided up into well-defined areas. A variety of toys and equipment were labelled and arranged in distinctive areas such that they were accessible to all. Materials were varied and open-ended in their functions; for example, there was always a place for 'found' or 'junk' material. Outside there were areas of different interest, for example, a picnic area, bird table, sand, wheelie toys and climbing frame.

Daily routine

Adequate time was set aside for 'planning, doing and reviewing' (this could last for two hours). Work-time was entirely child-led, and the role of the adult was to observe, follow and support. Children tended to settle into planning-time very quickly; however, it was usually quite a while before they actually related what a 'plan' was to what they actually did. The length of time required for a child to understand the concept of 'planning' usually varied according to the child's own development. The importance of striking a balance between small and large group activities was recognised by staff; before the introduction of High/Scope the Nursery Supervisor saw group sessions as more 'ad hoc' with a less holistic approach to the child's needs and experiences in the nursery.

Adult–child interaction

Staff encouraged problem-solving and independence and at the same time cooperation amongst children. They did 'let go' of some of the control and became more aware of how they talked to children. Staff extended and encouraged language through participation, playing 'alongside' the children and encouraging conversation about their activities. A balance of responsibility was achieved; children initiated activities during work-time while adults initiated acts during small-group time. The children gained a sense of security from knowing that every day the adult would provide a planned activity which the child could explore in his or her own way. The High/Scope adult presented the activity (usually during small-group time) and then waited to see how the children responded: only then did she ask questions, comment or provide support. The High/Scope Trainer illustrated this by example:

> 'An adult sits for three-quarters of an hour, *not* doing a jigsaw for a child, "because it's easier" but waiting and giving verbal support until the child, through trial and error, completes it independently.'

Adult–adult interaction

Each day, time was set aside to facilitate team teaching, planning, evaluation and feedback. Prior to the introduction of High/Scope the approach to planning sessions was usually more 'ad hoc'. Insofar as was feasible, assessment using the CAR and COR forms was carried out; in reality, time constraints hindered more regular commitment to this aspect of High/Scope. A variety of recording systems had been used over the years at the nursery prior to the introduction of High/Scope.

Home visits, which were an integral part of the early High/Scope programmes in the USA, were not fully implemented due to staff and time constraints. While the Nursery Supervisor admitted that the parental role in the nursery had not really changed to any extent since the introduction of High/Scope – staff had always recognised the contribution that parents can make in the education of their children – the introduction of a new curriculum opened up new avenues for discussion.

Daily routine

So what is a High/Scope nursery like? How do staff use the curriculum in practice? Here, we present a picture of daily life at Millbrook Nursery, illustrating how the children and staff interpreted the High/Scope concepts.

Each day the core elements of the curriculum were followed with each group (there were four groups in total), but not necessarily in the same order. While one group of eight children experienced the elements of High/Scope in a consistent order each day, another group of eight children may have had the same experiences but in a different order. The children were always in the same group for their activities. The key was consistency within groups.

The day began at 9.30 a.m. when the children arrived at the nursery. (They were collected from home by a bus which left the nursery at 8.30 a.m.) Much activity ensued with the children hanging up coats and using the toilet, followed by breakfast. This settling-in period usually lasted for about 30 minutes.

Circle-time was important, as each child was greeted and acknowledged in a special way. If there were going to be any changes in the daily routine, or if there was any new equipment to be shown, this happened during circle-time. Circle-time afforded children the opportunity of being 'centred' before starting the day's work.

Next, one group might start their plan/do/review while another might get involved in small-group work. In the plan/do/review sequence, planning could take anything up to 30 minutes, allocation of work-time an hour, and review anything from 15 to 30 minutes. Children could write down, draw out or even mime their plans. The length of time needed to learn to plan varied from one week to several, depending on the individual child. The Trainer felt that alert, observant adults could help a child to plan from the start by noticing a choice being made and acknowledging that choice. However, while most children settled very quickly into the planning-time it was usually quite a while before they learnt to relate what a 'plan' was to what they were actually doing. Again, the length of time was dependent on the individual child. Some children had more difficulty remembering their plans than others; some, according to the Nursery Supervisor, remembered exactly what their plans were and followed them through; others planned one thing and immediately headed off in another direction.

However, this skill in planning 'did improve with time'. Often when the children were coming into the nursery on the bus they were already planning their time. They may have chatted amongst themselves about what they were going to do that day or informed the adult(s) present. Indeed, the Nursery Supervisor reported that parents often told her how their children were already planning what they were going to do at pre-school each day while they were getting dressed in the morning. Furthermore, children who may not have appeared to be very interested in planning during 'planning-time' had often already done their planning and hence knew what they would be doing that day: 'They seemed more aware of the options open to them and were really thinking about what they wanted to do with their time instead of "flitting"' (Nursery Supervisor). The children learnt that it was quite acceptable to change their plans so long as they acknowledged this at the time.

High/Scope's child-centred approach fostered an 'encouraging' rather than 'coercive' attitude. For example, if a child chose not to participate, staff came to regard this as acceptable and, rather than pushing the child, they would encourage him or her with a phrase such as, 'Perhaps you'll join us when you're ready'. The Trainer felt that High/Scope was more helpful in this regard than other curricula, as it acknowledges the right of children who want or need to opt out and gives staff permission to accommodate this within a clearly defined framework. In practice, according to the Nursery Supervisor, it was unusual for children not to want to get involved in the plan/do/review routine: 'Unless a child was experiencing difficulties I have found that they enjoyed the daily routine.' Planning gave children the opportunity to develop language and to learn the names of the areas and equipment. Their listening skills improved and they began to realise that they would be listened to and have their choices respected.

The 'do' part of the plan/do/review was different from work-time in other pre-school curricula in that it was entirely child-led. There was less emphasis on tidiness and more on 'doing' and 'exploring'. The Nursery Supervisor described one child's experience: 'She could really run the place, she knew exactly what the routine was, she was able to follow it, she interacted well with the other children and was quite bright and outgoing.'

Key experiences were quite obviously integrated into the children's learning activities. The High/Scope Trainer related an experience in another Barnardo's nursery in Dublin where High/Scope was introduced in the wake of its success at Millbrook:

'Children and adults were reading a story in which a pig featured. A conversation about rashers developed. All moved to the kitchen to see if there were any rashers. None. Undaunted the adult organised a trip to the shops – rashers were purchased and brought back to the pre-school, cooked and eaten.'

The immediate response here was vital. The key experiences included classification – the children discovered (or knew already) that rashers come from pigs; using language – describing the relationship between pigs and rashers; developing logical reasoning, in this case in relation to numeracy – the children saw the money being handed over to pay for the rashers and the change being handed back.

High/Scope work-time also differed from that time in other curricula in terms of level of activity:

'The level of activity appeared to be greater. The support given to the children during this time by staff was much more intensive. The level of choice and freedom to choose and explore was greater. The general level of movement within the group from area to area was different to other curricula I have experienced.'

Often, particularly in the early stages, children tended to repeat the same activities. Strategies chosen by staff to counter this tendency depended on the individual child. Children were encouraged to use all areas and equipment to facilitate their development. Small-group time was utilised to introduce new activities, and the children could then be reminded of these activities when it came to planning their own.

Tidy-up time was an important feature before reviewing could take place. This tended to take longer at the beginning of the year, until the children became familiar with the routines. All children were encouraged by the adults to clean up, and sometimes songs or games were used to make the process more enjoyable, for example singing 'It's time to tidy up', or 'Let's tidy all the yellow things first.'

Recall and review time allowed the children to settle down and to chat, as well as to remember what they had done. At first, getting the children to review was difficult for staff as they felt under pressure to ensure all the children had done this; however, when the Trainer suggested recalling with just one or two of the children it became easier, as then all the children became interested. By Christmas most of the children would have been reviewing at some level, and reviewing with ease during the summer term.

At approximately noon, the group who had had their plan/do/review were ready for small-group time (approximately 20 to 30 minutes) while those who had already had this time could play outside.

While other pre-school curricula also provide small-group time, the Trainer felt that the High/Scope teacher does not steer the children towards something to the same extent as teachers of other curricula. Instead, she or he presents the activity, waits to see how the children respond, and only then asks questions or makes comments.

Dinner-time lasted from 12.30 to 1.00 p.m. Outside-time constituted another important part of the day. Children who had not been outside, now had the opportunity until home-time at 1.30 p.m. Whereas other curricula often regard this period as a time for letting the children off to have a 'rest', the Trainer felt that High/Scope affords it more importance. During this time, activities centred around the picnic area, sand table, climbing frame and wheelie toys. Children's pretend play also developed as a result of staff involvement with the games. The High/Scope expectation is that adults can extend and encourage language through participation and playing 'alongside' the children. Lively boisterous play was channelled to the block area where the soft blocks offered a safe opportunity to 'let off steam' and move on to other activities. Adult fears that children would not use 'educational equipment' proved unfounded; the Trainer highlighted the learning which was occurring naturally through self-initiated play. The final part of the day was 'staff-time'; after the children had left, the staff group come together to review the day, monitor the children's developments and plan for the next day.

Following the High/Scope curriculum meant that the pre-school day was very structured. This structure involved transition periods from one activity to another. The Trainer reported that transitions from one stage in the day to the next were 'sometimes smooth, sometimes bumpy'. Movement from work to tidy-up time sometimes proved difficult: 'Usually the children were very involved at this time and tidy-up was not exactly their favourite time.' Such problems usually disappeared as the year progressed and children and staff became more accustomed to each other.

According to the Nursery Supervisor, the parental role did not change to any great extent with the introduction of High/Scope, although more information-sharing about the programme was necessary. Staff at the nursery had always recognised the value of parental participation: 'A central part of the work is building relationships with parents, as they do contribute to a great extent to our understanding of the child.'

However, major changes in the working relationship between staff were noted. Most noteworthy, according to the Nursery Supervisor, was that 'There was more of a "team approach" to working with the children'. In the early days of implementation there was more disruption, which the Trainer attributed to a sense amongst the staff of being deskilled. However, when the programme became established this sense decreased, and staff realised that things which had caused problems before – for example, some of the children not holding hands when walking in from the bus, or not replacing each piece of equipment immediately after use, or not wanting to do jigsaws when it was 'jigsaw time' – were no longer an issue because the attitudes and expectations of the staff had altered.

The extent of High/Scope implementation

Both Nursery Supervisor and High/Scope Trainer were asked to evaluate how much of High/Scope they felt had been taken 'on board' at the nursery. Both felt that the daily routine with its individual elements such as plan/do/review and small-group time had been fully implemented. The importance of an appropriate 'child friendly' room arrangement was also recognised and the necessary alterations were made accordingly. Daily team meetings were also facilitated. The Nursery Supervisor felt that overall, while regular assessment of children was not fully implemented due to factors such as pressure on staff members' time, this element was incorporated as much as was possible. Home visits were only partially implemented; this was due, again, to factors such as time pressure.

Case history: Paula, aged three years

Children who attended the nursery were referred because they were deemed 'at risk' by those concerned with their welfare – for example, social workers, psychologists, doctors. Many of these children were experiencing difficulties which, for the most part, were symptomatic of the kind of turbulent home environments in which they lived. In the following section the situation of a child at the nursery is related. To preserve confidentiality a fictitious child 'Paula' will be used. 'Paula' is a composite of some of the children in the sample group. Her story is told to illustrate the way in which High/Scope was used within Millbrook.

Paula's speech was delayed. Her mother was experiencing management difficulties and her ability to understand children's needs was limited. As a result, Paula's behaviour was most unsettled. There were problems in school with older siblings also. The family had experienced extensive disruption over the last few years, in particular the fact that there were different fathers in the case of three out of the four children.

Using High/Scope to help Paula to overcome her problems

The initial strategy was to enable her mother to recognise and acknowledge Paula's difficulties and to invite her to give a commitment to working with the staff towards solving them. This was achieved in a variety of ways. First, there was a home visit which enabled the reason for referral to be properly discussed; next the mother visited the nursery and its work was explained to her; she was also invited to attend the Parents' Group where issues relating to herself and her child could be addressed.

As already stated, High/Scope places much emphasis on the importance of the parental role in the education of the child. While home visits were not a central feature in Millbrook in the way that they were in the early US programmes, this was – as was mentioned earlier in the chapter – more due to time constraints than to any lack of acknowledgement of their importance by the staff.

At Millbrook, Paula's speech delay and behavioural problems were addressed. While Paula was referred to a speech therapist from the Eastern Health Board, she received as much one-to-one attention as was feasible from the pre-school staff, who found High/Scope particularly useful in addressing deficits in this area. The plan/do/review routine presented numerous occasions for Paula to talk both to adults and to other children. The pre-school teacher encouraged her to tell her plans to the other children and herself. It did not matter that her limited expressive language skills meant that her plans were basic, for example: 'Build with bricks'.

Paula was encouraged to speak at times other than the plan/do/review period; indeed throughout the day she was encouraged to speak freely about anything she was doing, observing or feeling. Staff encouraged active listening so that Paula would pick up vocabulary both from themselves and the other children. They listened to what she said – it did not matter that it may have taken her longer to say things than many of the other children – and spoke precisely to her, describing objects, events and relations, and responded to any interest she demonstrated in letters, sounds and words. Providing children with interesting things to explore and use is essential to the development of descriptive language. As already stated, the High/Scope environment places a good deal of emphasis on the importance of providing educational toys and equipment in the nursery.

Monitoring Paula's progress using the COR and CAR forms

In order to monitor Paula's progress, a COR form was completed at three points during the year – when Paula started at the nursery, midway through the year and at the end of the year. While all areas of Paula's progress were monitored, particular attention was paid to language and social/emotional development.

With regard to recording language development, a typical entry in the CAR form in September would have read: 'Paula showed the teacher her new shoes, by pointing to her feet and saying "new shoes".' Towards the end of the year a typical entry would have been: 'My Daddy brought me to school today because Mammy is sick.' Hence, an advance in her language was evident. As illustrated in Table 5.1, when the pre-school teacher completed the COR form at time period one she circled 2 in the expressive language area, whereas by the end of the year – time period three – she circled 3.

Table 5.1   Using language

	Basic expressive vocabulary	Time 1	2	3
(1)	Child only communicates in ways other than spoken language	1	1	1
(2)	Child uses a small number of words to communicate with adults and peers (eg 'Look it!' 'No!')	2	0	2
(3)	Child's spoken language is adequate for communication	3	3	0
(4)	Child's spoken vocabulary is large and varied	4	4	4

In order to address Paula's behavioural problems, clear messages were given to Paula about what constituted acceptable behaviour in the nursery. Adherence to High/Scope's daily routine provided a structure and consistency that was obviously lacking in her home life. The plan/do/review cycle helped to develop her concentration skills and encouraged her to complete the activities she had started. High/Scope's 'child choice' philosophy gave Paula a sense of control over her life. Furthermore, she was provided with opportunities to experience success and praise in her activities in the nursery; nursery staff hoped that this would help build up her self-esteem.

Paula's progress was monitored closely by nursery staff. High/Scope's COR form recorded her activities at regular intervals and the CAR forms recorded more specific instances of behaviour. For example, a typical entry on a CAR form in September would have been: 'Paula grabbed the jigsaw she wanted from Michael', whereas at the end of the year an entry in this area might have read: 'Paula played quietly on her own with beads, while waiting for Michael to finish his jigsaw.' When the pre-school teacher completed the COR form at period one she circled 1, but by the end of the year she circled 6. At the end of each term there was a review of Paula's progress, and plans for the following term were made by staff. Strategies were decided upon by staff and opportunities provided for her in those areas where 'low' numbers, for example 1 and 2, had been circled. These sessions also encouraged parental involvement.

Table 5.2   Social and emotional development

			Time	
	Relationships with peers	1	2	3
(1)	Child does none of the following	0	1	1
(2)	Child engages in parallel play	2	2	2
(3)	Child responds when peers initiate interaction	3	3	3
(4)	Child initiates interactions with peers	4	4	4
(5)	Child sustains interactions with peers	5	5	5
(6)	Child works with peers towards a common goal (eg sharing labour, abiding by common rules)	6	6	0

Conclusion

The aim of this chapter has been to provide the reader with an insight into the operation of High/Scope at Barnardo's in Tallaght. The specifics of how High/Scope was adopted for use there and how the children progressed with High/Scope have been investigated. This points to definite lessons that can be learnt from the experience in Tallaght:

- The importance of substantial input from the Trainer and the fact that the Trainer was 'on site' during the implementation process meant that learning about High/Scope was an ongoing process.
- Having a specific time set aside every afternoon to facilitate team teaching meant that the particular needs of each child could be more carefully identified; sessions were more focused, so staff gained much more from them.
- The fact that the physical structure of the room was rearranged and reorganised meant that children benefited from a spacious room arrangement which allowed them to explore freely without any concerns for their safety, giving them ready access to toys and equipment.
- Some elements of the High/Scope curriculum were particularly

important for the children's cognitive development, for example, the plan/do/review routine had many inherent benefits for the child – language development, development of logical reasoning, development of memory skills.

- The experience of using High/Scope led to altered attitudes and expectations on the part of staff; this meant that previous problems – such as the child not wanting to do a jigsaw during the allocated jigsaw-making time – no longer arose as activities were now much more child-initiated rather than directed by an adult.

- Experience suggests that it is not necessary to adopt all the elements of the High/Scope curriculum at once in order to provide a good quality pre-school experience for children. Adopting High/Scope as a more phased process, with new elements being adopted over time and existing elements being modified to suit individual needs, may be advantageous.

Finally, a composite of cases, 'Paula', was presented to give the reader an idea of the degree of disadvantage experienced by the children at the nursery and to illustrate how High/Scope can be used to address these issues. In the following chapter the children's progression during the year at the nursery and in the two years following, is described.

6. Assessing the impact of High/Scope

This chapter is an evaluation of High/Scope in the broadest sense. We draw together information from several sources and perspectives to assess the use of the High/Scope curriculum in the nursery and the impact on children as they move through the early years of schooling. We present data from different sources, starting with the perspectives of the staff at Millbrook Nursery – what they thought of the High/Scope curriculum, the manner in which it was introduced and its effect on the children. Next we consider parents' views. Then the opinions of the primary school teachers regarding the academic performance and social and emotional behaviour of the children (both those who had experienced High/Scope and those who had not) will be investigated. Throughout the three years of the study, specific quantitative data was collected to monitor the progress of the High/Scope group in terms of both academic and social assessment measures. Similar data was gathered on children in the contrast group over two years. Evaluative results are described briefly in this chapter (and in more detail in Appendix B).

The perspectives of the nursery staff

As part of the evaluation of the High/Scope programme it was important to ascertain the views of the nursery staff. This was achieved through formal interviews with the High/Scope Trainer, the Project Leader and the Nursery Supervisor, together with informal feedback gained through observation, through discussion of each child's progress and in particular by focusing on their COR forms and by noting the reactions of both staff and children to the videos of nursery activity. Comments on the staff's initial impressions of High/Scope, its impact on the nursery and its effects on relationships with parents are outlined below.

Initial impressions of High/Scope

The High/Scope Trainer was initially, by her own account, a sceptical participant in the training. However, what emerged in the course of her training was an affirmation that High/Scope supported the kind of work in which she had already been engaged. It highlighted an approach that integrated other elements she had been taught or learnt through experience, validating and formalising them. The drawing together of other approaches was a particularly useful aspect of High/Scope and it offered her considerable balance of approach towards good nursery practice. She described High/Scope's specific and explicit focus on the role of the adult and the genuine sharing of control, supported by a structure which reviews and records adults' and children's work, as the elements which make High/Scope different. She saw the primary purpose of High/Scope, from the point of view of the adult, as identifying and presenting as a package the kinds of activities and experiences that children need, in order to ensure that they are receiving good-quality pre-schooling.

The Nursery Supervisor's initial impression was positive. She was enthusiastic because High/Scope was the only pre-school programme, to her knowledge, that had been validated to a certain extent by research evidence, especially as it was regarded as particularly suitable for children from disadvantaged areas. Hence, she felt that it would present the staff with an approach appropriate to the children with whom they were working. Furthermore, she considered it attractive because it appeared to provide a uniform programme for use by all staff and children at Millbrook. Since the same problems tended to arise for everyone, the new curriculum provided a cohesive framework for the staff within which they could resolve them. Prior to the introduction of High/Scope, as staff were from a variety of professional backgrounds, a mixture of approaches had been evident. Consequently, input from staff varied from group to group, with individual groups of children often having quite different experiences. While the range of materials and layout would have been the same for all groups, there had been a very loose curriculum structure.

The impact of High/Scope on the children at the nursery

In her evaluation of High/Scope the Nursery Supervisor was particularly impressed that the children appeared more settled overall than in the period prior to implementation. Another major benefit of the High/Scope programme was the reduced impact of staff absences on the children. Previously, when a staff member was absent, children had to join with another group who did things differently from their own, and they often found this lack of continuity distressing. Now if a staff member was absent, making it necessary for the children to join in with another group, they did not experience any loss of security because all staff were using the same curriculum and hence staff approaches and expectations were the same.

High/Scope's effects on negative behaviour were also impressive. If a child was disruptive or aggressive the structure of the curriculum and the child-centred focus enabled staff to indicate that this was unacceptable and a plan to do something constructive was suggested.

'I have seen children who started in the programme by climbing on furniture, knocking equipment off shelves and walking on shelves reach a point where they sat, pencil and paper in hand, "recording" plans at planning time.' (High/Scope Trainer.)

'I think he learned that he just couldn't do what he liked basically, that the limits were set for him and that he had to stay with them. That was a huge preparation for him. He came on a lot in different areas of development ... his level of play, social and instructive, was much more advanced. The main focus was to teach him to observe the boundaries that were set for him and I think that was achieved.' (Nursery Supervisor.)

The way children learnt to relate to each other and to adults was seen as a major development:

'He did come on and was able to relate quite well to "X" [pre-school teacher] and form relationships with other children.'

'The fact that he built up a relationship with "Y" [pre-school teacher] was a great achievement because he had been quite hostile.'

Another feature of the High/Scope curriculum clearly identified by the Nursery Supervisor was the fact that the programme reduced the level of chaos at the beginning of term, such that the children fitted in and adapted remarkably quickly. For example in referring to one of the children, 'She knew exactly what the routine was and she was able to follow it.'

Similarly the Project Leader felt that one of the main benefits of the High/Scope curriculum was the fact that the children adapted very well to the routine. Their alertness to which stage of the programme was next was always evident to staff, reflecting the children's need for routine and their enthusiasm for it. Both Trainer and Nursery Supervisor were agreed that High/Scope 'graduates' had a greater ability to use their initiative and make decisions than children who had not had such pre-school experience. They also felt that the High/Scope 'graduates' had an increased ability for self-expression and for working with other children and adults to solve problems. In most cases the children had better self-discipline. Language was another area of development where improvements were noted. The Project Leader recalled how the duration and quality of recall time became extended and noticeably more elaborate in content for all of the children as the year progressed. Indeed, by the end of the year it was apparent to nursery staff that the children were ready to begin primary school: 'Certainly by the time she left she was well ready for school.' 'I think that by the time he left he was just streets ahead of where he would have been at, going straight into school.'

We shall return to this issue when we examine the results of the psychometric tests with the children.

Effects on staff–parent relationships

Staff had always found that engaging the cooperation of parents meant that they were generally more positive and less defensive. Moreover, the quality of staff/parent relationships influenced the children's progress at the nursery. The Nursery Supervisor detailed the case of working with one family for whom circumstances were particularly poor:

> 'We found the family very responsive to work with and I developed very good relationships with the mother while they were here, and really they were very cooperative in anything we asked them to do. I think the child did really well while he was here ... By the end of the year I think he had come on really well, albeit in the last two months and he was great by the time he left.'

High/Scope has become integrated into Barnardo's service in that it provides a positive focus for working in partnership with parents. This positive focus has provided a strong impetus for the establishment of the parent groups at the nursery and the emergence of the after-school groups.

The manner in which High/Scope was introduced

Earlier in this text we described the introduction of High/Scope to Millbrook; here we assess some of the effects of that process. One of the most immediate advantages that High/Scope offered was funding. No other form of funding of such a substantial nature existed for the service provided by the nursery at Millbrook. However, interviews conducted with staff during the first year of the evaluation revealed that while High/Scope had many inherent advantages which would be directly beneficial for them, there were teething difficulties.

With the implementation of High/Scope the staff in Millbrook were required to work more as a team, to undergo training and to subject their own work to continuous examination. The early days saw most disruption, as already mentioned in Chapter 5; the Trainer attributed this to a sense amongst the staff of being de-skilled. Furthermore, the introduction of High/Scope was viewed primarily as a management decision imposed on staff. There was a natural defensiveness related to the fact that they had to take on the process without knowing fully what it involved, or how it was any better than what they were already using. Initially, there was a feeling of 'We're doing alright', and a degree of reservation about the need to change. Indeed, it might have been said that such a change was an inherent criticism of what went before, and that staff were being observed and evaluated in a way which was unlike anything in their previous experience.

There were other specific aspects of High/Scope to which staff found it difficult to adjust. The compromise between High/Scope and Montessori approaches was an initial stumbling-block, as some members of staff were very committed to a Montessori approach. For example, Montessori-trained teachers had always encouraged a degree of child choice, but with High/Scope this choice was more unconditional. In a Montessori nursery the children might be given certain shapes to explore. In a High/Scope nursery the children might be allowed the choice of whether or not they wanted to work with shapes or something else that morning. Working within a shared area, as opposed to each having their own domain, was just not attractive for some staff members. Furthermore, the programme was perceived by some as being almost independent of personal input which was a difficult concept to accept. Despite these concerns, the Nursery Supervisor summarised the reactions of the staff as follows:

'They felt that there wasn't a large difference in the High/Scope philosophy in comparison to what we were already using and that what it meant for them was just some changing in the structure of the day, but they all liked the philosophy involved. That really made it work. I don't think people would have bought into it otherwise.'

Having the full-time support of a trainer on site was obviously important, although, when asked what she felt was the most stressful aspect of the process, the Trainer replied: 'Working two steps ahead of staff who were not clear of what was really expected of them to begin with.' She also commented that the written planning and recording aspect of the High/Scope curriculum meant a lot more preparation and review time for staff. She felt that this was an extra drain as time had to be set aside to do this. However, the opportunity for staff at the nursery to meet together every afternoon to reflect on the day and think about the needs of each child contributed significantly to the quality of the service they were able to offer the children.

The Project Leader felt that many initial problems arose because Barnardo's were the first organisation in Ireland to implement the programme. There was no High/Scope Centre in Ireland to visit or to use as a yardstick against which to measure what was being attempted at Millbrook. She felt that the main difficulty that staff experienced was that they were unable to take 'time out' for training. Everyone was learning at the same time – pre-school workers, Supervisor, High/Scope Trainer and managers at Barnardo's. Indeed, the Trainer agreed that the inclusion of a formal induction process involving all staff members from the outset would have been useful. Ideally, the Nursery Supervisor would have preferred to have attended a training course in High/Scope prior to implementation of the programme. The Project Leader also referred to the fact that staff were required to undergo feedback sessions on performance and to try to assimilate new material late in the afternoon having already completed their day's work. Sessions were inclined to be rushed at this time and staff were understandably tired.

Observations made by a former project leader at Tallaght concerning the later introduction of High/Scope to another Barnardo's nursery in Blanchardstown in Dublin illustrated that the whole manner in which this was achieved contrasted sharply with the process that the Trainer described at Tallaght. There, staff were asked to attend an introductory course about High/Scope, encouraged to evaluate the High/Scope approach for themselves and to discuss their views having taken the course. The transition stage was much more gradual and tight time-scales were not involved. Unlike the situation at Tallaght where implementation was sudden, much discussion and dialogue preceded High/Scope at Blanchardstown. When asked what advice she would give to anyone thinking of adopting High/Scope, the Trainer replied:

'Take it easy, start with whatever aspect of the programme feels most manageable. Be prepared for ups and downs and a sense of being deskilled – experience of others is useful to draw on. Use your

High/Scope book and draw on each others' strengths. Talk about problems as they arise and discuss them.'

In sum, qualitative data, gained from nursery staff, revealed that despite initial teething problems, there was satisfaction with the process overall, with an excitement about the contents of the curriculum and its anticipated effects on the children. The Trainer was impressed that the curriculum, in addition to having many interesting and specific features, also incorporated important elements of other high-quality curricula. The nursery staff felt the curriculum to be particularly suitable for the children for whom the nursery catered in terms of consistency in approach and the limits it provided for them, which translated into positive effects with respect to their social/emotional development.

Parent evaluations of High/Scope

The curriculum

Although introducing a new curriculum to the nursery necessitated more information-sharing with the parents about what the programme involved, the Nursery Supervisor felt that the parental role did not change to any great extent following the introduction of High/Scope. It was intended to interview all the parents about their perceptions of their children's progress in general, their perceptions of the advantages/disadvantages of the High/Scope curriculum, and the extent to which they perceived themselves to have benefited from the work conducted at the nursery. Despite the efforts of the staff and research team only a small number of parents agreed to be interviewed. The impression formed was that they did not really have a picture of what the High/Scope curriculum involved as distinct from any other form of pre-school curriculum. When one mother was asked for her comments she replied: 'Just a general pre-school programme is my picture. Just to help them plan, make decisions for themselves, that's about it really.' Although this mother may not have seen High/Scope as anything different, her comment suggests that the concept of planning and taking responsibility had been understood. Another, a mother of three children, demonstrated greater awareness of High/Scope: 'I can see a big difference between the oldest girl and the two that had this High/Scope.'

As regards children's progress all parents were enthusiastic, affirming and positive about the work conducted at the nursery. All of the parents perceived their children's needs to have been met. One parent, when asked how she felt about the nursery, responded:

> 'Absolutely brilliant, he's been here two years now. Last May–June he was reviewed for school but he wasn't ready. He just couldn't mix – very good in other ways but just couldn't mix. So we said we'd just give him another year and within three months he'd just changed completely. Before that, you'd just bring him into a room and he'd just stand there and wait to be invited.'

Attendance at the nursery helped one mother who was experiencing separation difficulties with her child and indeed child-rearing/management difficulties in general. When asked if she felt that High/Scope had affected their relationship, she replied:

> 'I think it helped me a lot as well. For ages I couldn't do anything with him. He would just follow me everywhere, couldn't do anything without me. Now, I think he just trusts me, that I'm coming back, when he's dropped in the mornings. He's become so independent.'

Improvements in this regard were highlighted by a high proportion of parents. One mother commented, for example:

> 'He's improved a hell of a lot. He's come out of himself. He was very clingy towards me. I couldn't move outside the door. Come to think of it, I wouldn't even walk from here to the kitchen before.'

Other benefits noted by parents included the acquisition of concrete knowledge by the children. This was reflected in the way they could occupy themselves constructively at home. One parent enthusiastically commented:

> 'He even knows his shapes and knows stories. He's been bought books for his birthday and enjoys them. In that sense, he knows a hell of a lot. They've been very good to him. He knows his numbers, his ABC... and that's a good start, it really is.'

Another parent referred to the way her child had developed an understanding of the concept of time, as a result of being at the nursery:

> 'Especially at weekends or a Saturday in the middle of something else he'd say, "If I was in the nursery we'd be having cleaning up time by now," and in the morning he talks about what he'll be doing for the day!'

Understanding time and space is at the heart of the High/Scope curriculum. It is apparent that parents were indeed witnessing the benefits of High/Scope although they may not have realised that such characteristics are specific to the High/Scope curriculum.

In sum, parents were enthusiastic and positive in their opinions about the nursery. While the majority did not recognise the value of High/Scope as such (as distinct from any other pre-school curriculum), there was a definite awareness of how attending the nursery had benefited their children. They reported their children to have gained independence and maturity. They recalled how pre-school approaches did not end when they arrived home – children were often seen to be planning and working in just the same way as they would have been during the day!

Parent's views of the children's progress at school

Attempts were made to interview parents of both Group A and Group B children after the children had completed one year of schooling. Only a small number of parents – three in each case – agreed to be interviewed and, probably as could be expected, all were quite positive about their children's progress at school. From their reports it appears that the children had experienced little difficulty in settling into school. The following is a brief account of interviews conducted with mothers of children who had attended the High/Scope nursery.

Children were reported to be very independent and to have settled into school very quickly. Attendance at the nursery was the reason put forward for this. According to one mother, her child had progressed 'brilliantly' during his first year at school and had even helped the weaker members in the class: 'He gives her a lot of help in the class... he helps the teacher to help them.' Another child had got on 'very well' especially considering that he had gone to an all-Irish speaking school from an English-speaking pre-school. Mothers reported that their children liked to do things for themselves if possible, for example washing, dressing and preparing themselves for school in the mornings. No particular difficulties were expressed with regard to communication skills. One mother reported that 'If there is anything he doesn't understand he keeps asking ... he really thinks things through'.

Like Group A mothers, those mothers of Group B children who were interviewed also reported that their children had settled into school quickly and were very independent. One of these children had attended a Barnardo's community playgroup one afternoon each week the year prior to starting primary school and was involved in the toy library service; another had attended a local pre-school (not run by Barnardo's) for the two years prior to entering primary school, which consisted of three days a week the first year and four days a week the second year, and had also used Barnardo's toy library service. Another had attended a pre-school four mornings a week for five to six months in the year prior to starting school and had also been involved in Barnardo's toy library service. Mothers gave mixed accounts of their children's language skills: 'You have to talk babyish to him', 'People that know him can understand him', and 'I can understand him because I'm used to him.'

Primary teacher perspectives

One of the goals of the research was to investigate if the children who had experienced High/Scope were any more prepared for school than those who had not. Primary teachers were also involved in objective testing of the children's comprehension and behaviour, as reported in the next section. In addition, teachers were interviewed – those of both Group A (the High/Scope group) and Group B (the contrast group) children – towards the end of the first and second years of schooling. Analysis of the information collected indicated no apparent differences in functioning between the two groups. Some children in both groups were functioning well in each area – social/emotional, language and academic – while others in both groups were functioning poorly in one or more areas. For example, with regard to social/emotional behaviour there were some positive comments about individual Group A children made by teachers: 'Socially, always joins in. Very independent, organised, likes rules, structure – very mature', and some negative: 'He can be abusive, demanding'. Similarly, reports from teachers of Group B children were mixed, from 'Pleasing child, gets on well with everyone', to 'Has no relationships with the other kids'. Similarly with regard to language development and academic performance, teacher responses were mixed for children from both groups.

Educational and psychological assessments

Aims and design

A range of educational and psychological assessments were conducted at three points in the research study. The tests aimed to answer two key questions. To what extent was the High/Scope Curriculum successful in facilitating children's transition to primary school? How were the children who had experienced High/Scope performing in primary schooling as compared to peers who had received no or other kinds of early intervention?

These issues will be explored by reviewing and analysing data from two sources:

- Child Observation Record form data (as detailed in Chapter 3);
- Psychometric data.

The general aim of the Child Observation Record (COR) form data was to investigate if there was a difference in the overall functioning of Group A children in a positive direction over the course of their year at the High/Scope nursery.

The aims of the psychometric data collection and analysis were to:

(i) Assess the cognitive, language and social/emotional functioning of the children towards the end of the year 1991–2 at the nursery. This was to provide a baseline against which to compare functioning at two later stages – during the first year of primary schooling and during the second year – and will be referred to as round one data.

(ii) Assess Group A's performance as compared to a contrast group of children, Group B, at two points in time:
    – towards the end of the first year of primary schooling;
    – towards the end of second year of primary schooling.
    This data will be referred to as round two/first stage and round two/second stage data.

(iii) Monitor Group A's progress, in particular during their first two years of primary schooling.

Results of assessments

Round one

Round one refers to data collected when the children (Group A) were in the pre-school. The purpose of data collection at this stage was twofold. First, to establish a baseline in terms of how the children were functioning – cognitively/academically, socially and emotionally – against which to compare their performance one year later, on completion of one year of primary schooling, and again two years later. Establishing this baseline also meant that staff could see if children were ready to start school, and if children were making progress in pre-school.

General development: analysis of COR form data pertaining to the 22 children about to enter primary schooling indicated that performance improved from the initial to the last assessment periods. By and large this difference in a positive direction was as would be expected, since it is a characteristic of normal developmental functioning that children improve over time. According to scores obtained on the Vineland Adaptive Behaviour Scales (described in Appendix A), which assessed development in such areas as communication and personal care, the majority of children were found to be functioning at an adequate level (see Table 5, Appendix B).

Cognitive/academic development: analysis of scores on the cognitive measure (British Ability Scales) indicated that the group of children were functioning at average level. However, the range of scores (from minimum to maximum) indicated that some children were scoring substantially below average while others were scoring substantially above. With respect to the Goodenough-Harris Drawing Test scores, 12 children scored below the average on this test, while eight scored above it. With respect to language development, results obtained on the Reynell Developmental Language Scales indicated that, overall, the group of children were functioning at a level which is normal for children of this age with regard to both understanding language and expressing themselves. Furthermore, the range of receptive language scores, from minimum to maximum, indicated that some children were scoring substantially below the average (one child obtained a receptive language score of 2:10 years (two years 10 months)) while others were scoring above it (one child obtained a receptive language score of 5:10 years). The same was true for expressive language scores, with one child obtaining a score of 2:08 years and another an expressive language score of 5:01 years. (For a detailed description of the British Ability Scales, the Goodenough-Harris Drawing Test and the Reynell Developmental Language Scales see Appendix A. For score tables, see Appendix B).

Social/emotional functioning: the mean score obtained on the Behaviour Screening Questionnaire (see Appendix A for description) was calculated and indicated that, as a whole, the children were not presenting with behavioural problems. Furthermore, only one of the group of 22 was found to score above the cut-off point of 11 (which indicated that the child's behaviour required specialist clinical attention). See table 6, Appendix B.

Together these results indicate that, as a group, these children were progressing well, were functioning at an average level and demonstrated a readiness to move on to primary school.

These results are very encouraging. Indeed, given that the children come from an area of high social and economic disadvantage, and that each had identified individual problems, the results are better than would have been expected. The research design is not capable of demonstrating a direct causal relationship between these outcomes and the use of the High/Scope curriculum. However, taken together all the evidence suggests that the input of good-quality early years education has been important in protecting this group of children from early educational disadvantage.

Round two/first stage

Round two/first stage refers to data collected during both Group A and Group B children's first year of primary schooling. Data was collected at this stage for two reasons; first, to assess how well Group A children were progressing in school as compared to the previous year and, secondly, to assess their performance in comparison to children who had not experienced High/Scope (Group B). Results from the quantitative data collected indicate that there were no significant differences between the two groups of children, as assessed during their first year at primary school in any of the following areas.

Cognitive ability: analysis of results on the cognitive measure (British Ability Scales) indicated no overall significant differences between Group A and Group B. Furthermore, Group A children were functioning within average range in all but one of the areas (performance on the verbal comprehension scale was just slightly below what one would expect). Their range of scores on each subscale from minimum to maximum indicated that some children were scoring substantially below the average while others were scoring substantially above it (see Table 7, Appendix B). Group B children were also scoring within the average range in each area. As with the scores obtained by Group A, the range of scores indicated that some children were scoring substantially above average on some tests, while others were scoring substantially lower (see Table 8, Appendix B).

Social/emotional functioning: the majority of children exhibited no evidence of emotional or behavioural problems as assessed by the Preschool Behaviour Checklist (described in detail in Appendix A). A more detailed analysis of the scores is given in Table 11, Appendix B. Looking at the children's measured self-esteem, no significant differences were found between the two groups on each of the four scales – cognitive competence, peer acceptance, physical competence and maternal acceptance – of the Perceived Competence and Social Acceptance Scales (see Appendix A for full description of scales). Furthermore, children from both groups were found to have quite high opinions of themselves in these areas (see Table 9, Appendix B). Similarly, no significant differences were found between the two groups' teachers with respect to their evaluations of the children's *actual* competence and acceptance (see Table 10, Appendix B).

Round two/second stage

Round two/second stage refers to data collected towards the end of the children's second year of primary schooling. Data was collected at this stage in order to see how the High/Scope group had progressed since the previous year, and to compare once again the High/Scope group's and the contrast group's performance during their second year of primary schooling.

Cognitive development: analysis of results on the cognitive measure (British Ability Scales) indicated no overall significant differences between Group A and Group B children. Further analysis of group means on individual scales indicated no significant differences between the two groups on each of the four individual scales – matrices, similarities, recall of digits, naming vocabulary (see Appendix A for description of scales). Group A children were functioning within average range in all areas. Their range of scores from minimum to maximum indicated that some children were scoring substantially below the average while others were scoring substantially above it (see Table 12, Appendix B). Group B children were also scoring within the average range in each area. As with the scores obtained by Group A, the range of scores indicated that while some children were scoring substantially above average on some tests, others were scoring substantially lower (see Table 13, Appendix B).

Failure to complete the tests meant that it had not been possible to obtain an IQ score during stage one for two children – one from Group A, one from Group B. However, during stage two, the Group A child obtained an IQ score within the average range, while the Group B child was scoring below average. Two children (one from Group A and another from Group B) were scoring below average at both stage one and stage two.

Social/emotional functioning: analysis of the Children's Behaviour Questionnaire (described in Appendix A) revealed that the average score for both groups on problem behaviour was high. However, this is somewhat misleading as, in both cases, there were high mean scores because some children in each group had very high scores which 'dragged up' the average score. (See Table 17, Appendix B for information on standard deviation and minimum and maximum scores.) Furthermore, more children in each group were found to be exhibiting antisocial than neurotic traits (see Table 18, Appendix B). With respect to the Prosocial Behaviour Questionnaire (described in Appendix A), analysis of differences between group means indicated no significant differences. Where a score of 40 represented maximum prosocial score, Group A obtained a mean score of 22.33 and Group B a mean score of 20.58 (see Table 16, Appendix B). Looking at children's measured self-esteem, no significant differences were found between the two groups on each of the four scales of the Perceived Competence and Social Acceptance test – cognitive competence, peer acceptance, physical competence and maternal acceptance (see Table 14, Appendix B). Similarly, no significant differences were found between the two groups' teachers with respect to their evaluations of the children's *actual* competence and acceptance (see Table 15, Appendix B).

Comparison with previous evaluations of High/Scope
Research design

As with the Perry Preschool Project and the High/Scope Preschool Curriculum Comparison studies described in detail in Chapter 1, considerable lengths were taken in the present study to ensure the comparability of the research groups – those who attended the High/Scope nursery and the contrast group who did not. Our sample group was taken from deprived backgrounds and was made up of children who, as a consequence of their impoverished socio-economic backgrounds and identified personal problems, were at risk of educational disadvantage.

Unlike Weikart's study of 1962 in which the basic experiment was able, through random allocation, to contrast children who attended pre-school with children who had no pre-school experience, our contrast group had some kind of pre-school experience. Each group of children involved in the High/Scope Preschool Curriculum Comparison Study had experienced distinct kinds of pre-schooling differentiated primarily by the degree of initiative expected of the child and the teacher. It should also be noted that while the children in both the Perry Project and the High/Scope Curriculum Comparison study had two years of pre-schooling, the majority of our experimental group attended the pre-school for one year only.

Both the Perry Preschool study and the three curricula assessed in the High/Scope Curriculum Comparison study had two components – classroom sessions and educational home visits. In the Perry Preschool study, classroom sessions lasted for two-and-a-half hours, five days a week. A teacher visited each mother and child at home for 90-minute sessions every two weeks. Classes consisted of either 15 or 16 three- and four-year-olds. The typical pupil–teacher ratio was 1:8 for each of the three curricula groups and approximately 1:6 for all groups involved in the Perry Pre-school Project. In the present study, however, while classroom sessions were held from 9 a.m. till 1.30 p.m. four days a week, and pupil–teacher ratios were usually 1:8 for each group, pressure on staff and time constraints meant that regular home visits were not made.

The Perry Preschool study boasts large sample numbers – 58 children enrolled in the Project and 65 control children (the children in the experimental group) entered pre-school in subgroups of about a dozen each, one wave a year for five years beginning in 1962. Unfortunately, the sample numbers in the present study are not as impressive – 20 High/Scope and 20 contrast children, by the completion of testing. Small numbers in any sample mean that while there may be arithmetic differences, statistically significant differences are difficult to attain, and this makes any generalisation of results more difficult.

The research questions

Our research design differs from that of the Perry Preschool study in that we did not compare our experimental group to a contrast group *before* they started school. Hence the data we collected at that point may only be used as a baseline record and as an indication of how well-prepared the children were for school. We can make no assumptions about how the children were doing in relation to other children who had no contact with High/Scope prior to starting school.

The research results

Preliminary results from the Perry Preschool study found that children who had attended pre-school scored significantly and substantially higher than the control group children on standardised tests administered in the spring of their first and second pre-school years. Results of testing carried out at the end of the first year of primary schooling indicated that children from the experimental group consistently had somewhat higher scores than children in the control group on aptitude and achievement measures, and teacher ratings of academic potential obtained at kindergarten through to fourth grade. While differences in measured aptitude as measured by the California Achievement Test (CAT) gradually diminished during the post-treatment period, differences in academic achievement between the experimental and control groups actually increased over time. Not only did the consistency of significant differences on CAT subtests increase from first to fourth grades, but the magnitude of the treatment effect grew steadily. These findings suggest that the pre-school experience prepared experimental group children to cope more effectively with school.

It is in the longitudinal study of these children that the most interesting results appear. The latest round of research was undertaken when the sample groups were aged 27 years. This showed significant differences in the level of criminal arrests, earnings and property wealth, early pregnancy and commitment to marriage.

Results of the High/Scope Curriculum Comparison Study are not so convincing. Subjects involved in the High/Scope Curriculum Comparison study experienced a rise in IQ of between 23 and 29 points in their first year of pre-schooling which moved them out of the 'at risk' category. However, when all follow-up IQs (from ages four to ten) were averaged to give a mean IQ over time, the three pre-school curriculum groups did not differ significantly. Furthermore, the comparison of the three pre-school curriculum models yielded scant evidence that the models were differentially effective in improving children's intellectual performance. However, it was in the domain of longer-term social/emotional functioning that the most interesting and significant findings came to light. With regard to social behaviour, the Distar group engaged in twice as many delinquent acts as did the other two curriculum groups. Other areas of social behaviour corroborated this pattern of relatively poor social performance by the Distar group; for example poor family relations, less participation in sports or school job appointments. For most of the variables the sharpest contrast was with the High/Scope group, whose social behaviour was relatively positive.

Schweinhart and colleagues (1986) suggested a variety of possible reasons for the failure to find significant differences between the three curricula in terms of academic results in the short-term. First, lack of attainment of statistical significance may be explained by the small sample size; group differences even as large as 30 percentage points can fail to achieve statistical significance with such small sizes. In a sense, the small sample size is the price that has to be paid for tight experimental control, carefully controlled treatment conditions, and a decade-long longitudinal follow-up. The same could be said for this present study, which as already stated, was similarly limited in terms of small numbers. Although Weikart and colleagues employed intelligence tests these were not considered to measure innate abilities. Indeed, they measured performance on many tasks that are outside the cultural experience of poor and minority group children. Their rationale for using them was that they would be good indicators of programme effectiveness in preparing children to meet the demands of typical school settings. The same could be said about the educational and psychological measures used in the present study.

Comparing the research results

The results of the present study indicated no statistically significant differences at the end of the first year of primary schooling on:

- a measure of cognitive ability, except for two subscales – visual recognition and verbal comprehension – where the contrast group actually performed significantly better than the experimental group;
- a measure of social functioning, except for one item where the experimental group were found on average to be responsive to all staff and the contrast group were found on average to be somewhat withdrawn from all staff or responsive to only one staff member;
- a measure of perceived competence and social acceptance.

Similarly, at the end of their second year of primary schooling, no significant differences were found between the two groups on the same measures.

How can we explain the present study's non-significant results in the light of the impressive findings of the Perry study? First, unlike the Perry Project and the High/Scope Curriculum Comparison Study, we were not able to allocate children randomly so that one group experienced high-quality day care using the High/Scope curriculum while the other group received no early years service. Most of the children in the current contrast group also had some contact with pre-schooling (although we have no assessment of the overall quality of these varied experiences). It is likely that these experiences contributed to the overall development of the children in the contrast group so that they were more prepared for school than they would otherwise have been. Secondly, the current study is of a short duration compared to the longitudinal nature of the Perry project. There are no strong precedents for the findings obtained in the Perry Project and, indeed, the majority of compensatory pre-school studies with longitudinal follow-up report the attenuation of any achievement differences as time passes. Results from another Irish study (referred to in Chapter 2) carried out in a similarly disadvantaged part of Dublin city with children who would also be deemed to be 'at risk' of educational failure (O'Flaherty and others, 1994) did not yield quantifiable results in support of differential outcomes from good-quality pre-school intervention, any more than the present short-term quantitative results do.

What should be remembered is that statistically significant differences between the two groups involved in the Perry study were not as striking when the children were in the early years of primary education as later on. Similarly, while no differences in IQ and school achievement between the groups involved in the High/Scope Curriculum Comparison Study were identified in the short-term, at age 15 some differences in social variables – such as levels of delinquency and teenage pregnancy – did emerge in favour of the High/Scope and traditional nursery curricula. In the light of this, it is reasonable to suggest that our sample group may follow the same pattern.

Despite any measurably significant differences between the High/Scope group and the other pre-school group in the early years at school, the results from this current study are nonetheless encouraging. They show that a group of children from a highly disadvantaged area, all of whom have experienced additional individual problems, were functioning at the average level for their age-group and were well resourced to start school. In addition the results point to continuing cognitive, emotional and social development through early schooling.

Conclusion

The aims of this research study were set out in earlier chapters. These addressed four issues: the introduction of High/Scope into the nursery; the experiences of children at the nursery and their readiness for school; the progress of the children in their first two years at primary school; an assessment of how the children were functioning – cognitively, emotionally and socially – as compared to a peer group of children who had not experienced High/Scope. This book has reported on the findings generated by the research, focusing in this final chapter on the evaluation of High/Scope from a number of perspectives and using a range of measures. Here we summarise the main points again briefly.

• Despite some initial teething problems around the process of introducing High/Scope, overall the staff expressed an excitement about the contents of the new curriculum and its impact on the children. Of particular significance was the availability, on-site, of a full time trainer which was important in uniting a staff group from different childcare backgrounds.

- The evaluation suggests that the introduction of all the elements of High/Scope at once placed an unnecessary burden on the staff, who also felt insufficiently involved in the early decisions. Although High/Scope can be viewed as a package, it is possible to introduce the complete High/Scope curriculum in stages. The lessons from this first exercise were taken into account in the subsequent introduction of High/Scope into a second Barnardo's nursery in Dublin.

- The research indicated that the introduction of High/Scope had not only given the staff a structured and child-centred curriculum with clear aims, but it enhanced other aspects of the service – a system for record keeping and monitoring the development of the children; a well designed physical environment in which children could access resources; an emphasis on team teaching with time for staff to plan together to decide how best to meet the needs of each child.

- While parents expressed very positive views on the effect on their children from attending the nursery, there is limited evidence that they understood the significance of High/Scope.

- The children who attended the nursery were socially and economically disadvantaged and had been referred because of significant individual problems. Despite this predisposition to educational disadvantage, educational and psychological testing indicated that, after a year at the nursery, overall the children were performing well and within the norm for their age; this confirmed the assessment of staff that the children were well prepared for school. These results indicate that, against expectations, this group of children were able to start school on a par with their peers.

- The research did not find any statistically significant differences between the 'High/Scope' group and the contrast group in terms of their cognitive/academic, self-esteem, or socio/emotional functioning one or two years into school, although both groups of children were progressing well.

- These results obviously differ from those of the most significant High/Scope evaluation, the Perry Preschool study. However this is not entirely surprising for a number of reasons: this research project was much more limited in scale and length than the longitudinal American study – for instance the children, for the most part, had only experienced one year of the High/Scope curriculum rather than the two years of the Perry Project; the smaller sample numbers makes statistically significant differences less likely; it was not possible to randomly allocate children to groups, nor control the pre-school, but non-High/Scope, experiences of the contrast group.

- Furthermore the American research has revealed that it is during adolescence and early adulthood that the most significant differences emerge, primarily in areas such as achievement, motivation and social behaviour. Longitudinal research *may* demonstrate such differences between the two groups in this study at a later date, although caution must be exercised in making any such assumption, if only because American children are exposed to experiences which are culturally very different to those of Irish children.

- Finally, in reviewing the results from this research it is important to return to the issue of the *quality* of the early years experience. First, as highlighted in this text, most commentators would agree that good-quality early education depends upon a range of key indicators, which are not dependent solely on the use of a particular curriculum. Second, in assessing quality, it is equally important to focus on indicators of *process* as well as indictors of *outcome*. The evidence from this research suggests that the introduction of High/Scope into Millbrook enabled the children to experience high-quality early years education, in terms of stimulation, enjoyment and security – and to leave well prepared for school; such an experience is as important, in its own right, as subsequent differential measures of outcome.

Appendix A

Description of educational and psychometric instruments

Round one: instruments

Child Observation Record (COR) and Child Assessment Record (CAR)

COR forms were completed by the staff member most familiar with each child being assessed. The COR ratings were derived from daily, ongoing child assessment records (CAR forms) kept by programme staff. The information obtained from the CAR and COR forms had the advantage of being based on children's performance over a period of time. Since nursery teachers knew the children well, children who were nervous of the more formal testing situation were assessed more accurately on this continuous basis. A possible disadvantage, however, was bias among assessors. For example, there may have been a tendency for nursery teachers to show 'their' children to be making more progress than was actually the case.

Goodenough-Harris Drawing Test (Harris, 1963)

The Goodenough-Harris Drawing Test may be used to obtain an initial impression of a young child's general ability level. Children are requested to draw a picture of a man, then of a woman, and then of themselves. There is no time-limit for the test, but young children rarely take more than ten to 15 minutes for all three drawings. Each drawing is scored on the basis of whether or not it contains certain features, for example, if the head is present it gets a score of 1; if features alone are represented without any outline for the head itself it gets a score of 0. Hence each drawing yields a total score which is converted to a standard score that expresses the child's relative standing on the test, in relation to his or her own age- and sex group. Results may be used to select those children who should receive more detailed attention. The test may supply important additional evidence of severe intellectual and conceptual deficit. The Goodenough-Harris Drawing test was administered to each child at the nursery by a psychologist.

British Ability Scales (BAS) – revised short form (Elliot, Murray and Pearson, 1983)

The BAS is a standardised measure of intelligence (IQ). It was administered to the children at the nursery by the author. It differs from many other standardised IQ measures in that it is organised into a series of scales each of which measures a different aspect of a child's ability. An overall IQ score may also be calculated by averaging performance on the different scales. Six scales were chosen for use over the three years of testing in this project. A combination of four of these – visual recognition, verbal comprehension, naming vocabulary and recall of digits – was appropriate for children aged between two and five years. While a different combination – naming vocabulary, recall of digits, similarities and matrices – was administered to children aged between five and eight years.

(1) Recall of digits is a measure of short-term auditory memory. It is a test which requires the child to repeat (after the examiner) sets of digits in sequences ranging from two digits at a time up to nine. Short-term memory is obviously a requirement for the development of problem-solving skills; for example, a child cannot add two cars plus three trucks if he or she forgets how many cars he or she has been told there are.

(2) The Naming Vocabulary Scale consists of a booklet of pictures which the child is required to name (the pictures get progressively more complex). The aim of this test is to provide a measure of the child's language expression and vocabulary, so that the teacher will know more explicitly what skills are present and can be built upon, and also what language features are lacking.

(3) The Visual Recognition Scale is a measure of visual memory. It consists of a booklet of pictures and designs; the child is required to look at a picture of an object on one page and then to pick it out on another page where it is presented in a line-up of other pictures of objects. Again, visual memory is a necessary component of the development of problem-solving ability and is required in many classroom activities, for example, copying shapes and letters and eventually learning to write.

(4) The Verbal Comprehension Scale requires the child to follow simple instructions designed to test his or her understanding

of words such as, 'beside/under/behind'. This test aims to provide a measure of language understanding. Again it is essential that the child be able to understand what these terms mean if he or she is to follow instructions in the classroom situation.

(5) The Matrices Scale measures visual-motor reasoning. In simple terms, the child is presented with a series of designs with one part missing. The child is required to look at them and work out what the missing piece is and then to draw it in. Hence a facility for coordinating visual awareness, and appropriate drawing skills are required. Attention to detail and ability to draw patterns/shapes are components of many classroom activities. Hence, the importance of adequate development in this area.

(6) The Similarities Scale aims to assess verbal reasoning skills. A list of three items is read to the child, who is requested to state what the three items have in common. For example, the child is supposed to respond 'fruit' when a list such as 'orange, strawberry, banana' is called out. Lists of items become progressively difficult. Facility to label and categorise is an essential element of learning for the young child.

The advantage of a measure such as the BAS is that the possibility of bias among assessors is eliminated; an objective outsider administers the test. The most obvious possible disadvantage is the fact that the British Ability Scales test was standardised using British, not Irish children, so the test may not have taken adequate account of any possible cultural differences.

Reynell Developmental Language Scales – revised (Reynell, 1977)

These scales are intended to measure the child's receptive and expressive language. Receptive language is the child's ability to understand what is being said to him or her. Expressive, on the other hand, refers to the child's ability to communicate with others so that he or she may be understood. The Verbal Comprehension Scale attempts to follow the developmental progression of verbal comprehension without too much dependence on increasing the difficulty of the vocabulary used, and without increasing the sentence length excessively. The Expressive Language Scale is divided into three sections, each concerned with a different aspect of language. The earliest developmental stages (pre-symbolic) are included in section one; naming and the ability to describe word meanings in section two; and the use of language to express consecutive ideas in section three. Scores, if examined in the light of the individual patterns of scoring and the way in which the tasks are carried out, can give useful information on possible difficulties in verbal and expressive functioning.

The scales were developed in a clinical setting in response to an immediate need to assess language development in children with a mental handicap, and were used as a clinical tool throughout their development; this contrasts with the usual pattern of planning the whole scale, then carrying out pilot studies and standardising on a 'normal' sample, and finally applying the instrument clinically. After four years of trial and modification in a clinical setting, the scales were completely revised and standardised on a normal population. Hence the selection of questions and test material, the order of difficulty, the developmental stages and the separation of particular features for assessment were evolved in the course of clinical use. The Reynell Developmental Language Scales were administered to children at the nursery by a psychologist.

Vineland Adaptive Behaviour Scales (Sparrow, Balla and Cicchetti, 1984)

The Interview Edition of the Vineland was used. This is divided into four areas: daily living skills, socialisation, motor skills and communication skills and includes a section on maladaptive behaviour (for children five years and older). There are 297 items in total which are rated 2, 1, 0 in accordance with each child's strengths or weaknesses for each item. For example, a child's ability to use phrases or sentences containing 'but' and 'or' is one of the skills assessed. The revised Vineland requires a respondent who is familiar with the individual's behaviour, in this case, the nursery teachers. Like the CAR and COR forms, the Vineland has the advantage of being based on performance over a period of time. Similarly the main disadvantage is that bias among assessors may apply.

Behavioural Screening Questionnaire (Richman, Stevenson and Graham, 1971)

The Behavioural Screening Questionnaire was developed for use in screening pre-school children for behavioural disorders and developmental delay. It was completed with parents by a psychologist at the nursery. The obvious advantage of this measure is that it provides information on behaviour that might adversely affect school performance. In the present research it also complemented the Vineland, which was administered to nursery teachers, hence providing a complete account of the child's behaviour both at home and at school. Each item of the Behaviour Screening Questionnaire was scored on a scale of 0, 1, 2 enabling an overall score for each child's behaviour to be computed.

Round two/ first stage: instruments

BAS (as already described)
Perceived Competence and Social Acceptance (PCSA) (Harter and Pike, 1980)

This is a test designed to evaluate how children perceive their own competence – cognitive and physical – and how far children feel themselves to be accepted by both peers and their mothers. The PCSA test was administered to each child by the author (a psychologist) and took approximately 15 minutes per child.

There are male and female versions of the test. The test comprises four subscales – cognitive competence, physical competence, peer acceptance and maternal acceptance – each of which contains six items. There is also a sample practice item which is not scored. Half of the items are depicted with the more competent child on the left and described first, and half are depicted with the more competent child on the right. Within each subscale, three depict the competent child on the left, and three have that child on the right. Boys are shown pictures of boys, and girls pictures of girls. Two statements are read out about the pictures, for example, 'This girl/boy has lots of friends to play with'; 'This girl/boy doesn't have very many friends to play with', and the child is asked which one he or she is most like. Having selected one of the pictures the child is asked to indicate the degree to which he or she resembles the child in the picture, or in some cases the extent to which his or her mother is like the mother in the picture. (There is one large and one small circle underneath each picture to facilitate this – the child is required to point to the relevant circle in order to indicate degree of resemblance.) Each circle contains a number for scoring purposes.

Each item on the PCSA is scored from 1 to 4 depending on how positive a view the child has of him/herself (most positive = 4; least positive = 1).

The teacher rating scale was also administered. The teacher was asked to rate the child on the same dimensions and items to which the child was responding. Teachers were given a brief description of each activity and asked to rate how true it was for each child on a four-point scale. Teachers were asked to rate cognitive and physical competence as well as peer acceptance, excluding the the maternal acceptance items which they would probably not have been in a position to judge. Teachers rated their views of the child's actual competence and acceptance.

Preschool Behaviour Checklist (PBCL) (McGuire and Richman, 1988)

The PBCL is a quick screening device designed to help identify children with emotional and behavioural problems and, consequently, to help in the planning of intervention strategies to overcome these problems. It is intended for use with two- to five-year-olds. It allows staff to look at the severity as well as the incidence of a particular behaviour. The person completing the checklist (in this case the class teacher) is required to read each of 22 separate items. For each item there is a choice of descriptions, for example, an item designed to gauge the child's activity level includes four descriptive statements ranging from 'too active' to 'not active enough'. Each statement on the PBCL was scored 0, 1, 2 on the basis of severity. As a result of research in a number of nursery settings, a cut-off point of 12 has been set for the PBCL and it is likely that a child obtaining a score equal to or higher than this has behaviour problems which require further attention.

Round two/ second stage: instruments

BAS (as described earlier)
Perceived Competence and Social Acceptance Scale (as described earlier)

The Prosocial Behaviour Questionnaire (Weir and Duveen, 1980)

This is designed for use in the investigation of positive aspects of children's behaviour in primary school (aged five to 11 years). This questionnaire consists of a list of 20 statements about children's behaviour which may be shown by a child during the school day. The class teacher is requested to read each of the statements and, if the child definitely shows the behaviour described by the statement, to place a mark in the column headed 'certainly applies'. If the child exhibits the behaviour but to a lesser degree, or less often, he or she places the mark under 'applies somewhat'. If the child rarely or never shows such behaviour, the teacher is requested to place the mark under the column headed 'rarely applies'. The items are rated on a three-point scale: 'doesn't apply', 'applies somewhat', 'certainly applies' score 0, 1 and 2 respectively. A total score is derived from the addition of item scores. Class teachers of both groups completed this questionnaire during the period when the children were being assessed in school.

Children's Behaviour Questionnaire (Rutter, 1967)

This questionnaire investigates the presence of negative behaviour in children, covering behaviours similar to those investigated by the PBCL. The scale consists of 26 brief statements concerning the child's behaviour, to which the teacher has to check whether the statement 'certainly applies', 'applies somewhat' or 'doesn't apply' to the child in question. These are given a weight of 2, 1, and 0 respectively, to produce a total score with a range of 0 to 52 by summation of the scores of the 26 items. A 'neurotic' sub-score is obtained by summing the scores of four specific items, 'Often worried, worries about many things'; 'Often appears miserable, unhappy, tearful or distressed', 'Tends to be fearful or afraid of new things or new situations'; 'Has had tears on arrival at school or has refused to come into the building this year'. An 'antisocial' sub-score is obtained by summing the scores of six specific items, 'Often destroys own or others' belongings'; 'Frequently fights with other children'; 'Is often disobedient'; 'Often tells lies'; 'Has stolen things on one or more occasions'; 'Bullies other children'. The selection of children with neurotic or antisocial disorders by means of the scale is thus a two-stage procedure: (1) children with a total score of nine or more are designated as showing some behavioural disorder; (2) of these children, those with a neurotic score exceeding the antisocial score are designated 'neurotic', and those with an antisocial score exceeding the neurotic score are designated 'antisocial'. The children with equal neurotic and antisocial subscores remain undifferentiated. Teachers of both groups completed the questionnaire during the period when the children were being assessed in school.

Appendix B

Results of educational and psychological testing

Round one

COR form data

COR forms were examined for each child in order to identify the extent of progress in relation to nine dimensions – using language, representing, classification, seriation, number concepts, spatial relations, temporal relations, movement, social/emotional. Although it would be possible to aggregate scores on different dimensions, this is not the most appropriate use. Rather, scores are meant, in the present study, to supplement the results obtained on psychometric tests. Staff received feedback regarding how well children performed on the psychometric tests, and together with their knowledge gained from the COR records of how individual children were developing, were in a better position for planning for individual children.

General, cognitive and linguistic ability

Goodenough-Harris Drawing Test scores

A score of 100 represents a mean score; hence, a score of 120 indicates that a child is scoring substantially better than the average for his or her age- and sex-group. Two of the children did not complete this test. Of those who did, individual children were categorised according to how they scored in relation to the mean (see Table B1).

British Ability Scales scores

The results of the BAS are expressed as T scores. These scores allow an individual child's performance to be compared with other children of the same age. For each of the four scales – visual recognition, verbal comprehension, naming vocabulary and recall of digits – a T score of 50 indicates an average performance on that scale. A lower score indicates a performance that is poorer than

Table B1: Summary of Goodenough-Harris Drawing Test standard scores, categorised according to score range for 20 children

Scores	Score category			
	70–84	*85–99*	*100–115*	*116–130*
No. of children	2	10	4	4

Table B2: British Ability Scales scores

Scales	Mean score	Minimum -> maximum
Visual recognition	52.05	33 -> 67
Verbal comprehension	50.19	34 -> 61
Naming vocabulary	48	36 -> 68
Recall of digits	47.41	29 -> 65

average, and a higher score a performance that is better than average (see Table B2).

It was also possible to calculate overall IQ figures. These have a mean of 100. Nineteen of the children were found to be functioning at the mean or slightly above or below it. It was not possible to calculate an overall IQ score for one child, as only three scales had been administered; this was due to her limited capacity to concentrate. Hence, the majority of children were scoring at a level which is considered normal for children of their age-group. Table B3 presents the number of children in each score category. It can be seen that most children fall into the average range.

Table B3: British Ability Scales – score categories

No. of children	IQ score range	Level
1	121–131	Substantially above average
3	111–120	Above average
12	89–110	**Average**
4	79–88	Below average
1	68–78	Substantially below average

Reynell Developmental Language Scales scores

The mean chronological age and the mean receptive and expressive language scores were computed for 20 of the group of 22 and are presented in Table B4. (It was not possible to collect data from two of the children; one child had left the nursery prior to the scheduled administration and another's attention span proved too poor to continue with the test procedure.)

Table B4:   Receptive and expressive language scores

	Chronological age	Receptive language score	Expressive language score
Mean	4yrs 4mths	4yrs 6mths	4yrs 1mth
Minimum ->	3yrs 8mths ->	2yrs 10mths ->	2yrs 8mths ->
maximum	5yrs 4mths	5yrs 10mths	5yrs 1mth

Perusal of the table indicates that overall, the children were functioning at a level which is normal for children of this age, with regard to both understanding language and expressing themselves.

Social/emotional functioning

Vineland Adaptive Behaviour Composite scores

Raw scores for each of the four domains – communication, daily living skills, socialisation and motor skills – and for the final adaptive behaviour composite, were converted to standard scores. The resulting scores and the adaptive levels of the children are presented in Table B5. (Adaptive levels are based on ranges of standard scores and are intended to reflect, in words, the distance of each range of scores from the mean.) It is apparent from the table that the majority of children were functioning at an adequate level.

Table B5:   Vineland Standard Score Range and Adaptive Level

No. of children	Standard score range	Adaptive level
1	below 20 -> 69	Lo
5	70 -> 84	Mod lo
15	85 -> 115	Adequate
1	116 -> 130	Mod hi
0	131 -> above 160	Hi

Behaviour Screening Questionnaire

An overall score of less than 11 meant that there were no obvious behavioural difficulties causing concern. A score greater than 11 indicated that the child's behaviour was causing concern and hence may adversely affect school performance later on. The mean, standard deviation and range of scores are presented in Table B6.

Table B6: Mean and Standard Deviation Behaviour scores

Mean score	Standard deviation	Minimum –> maximum
5.73	3.03	1 –> 12

Round two/first stage: cognitive ability
British Ability Scales

Analysis of results on the cognitive measure (British Ability Scales) indicated no overall significant differences between Group A and Group B (t=–1.08, df 33, p>.05). However, if we take the mean IQ score to be 100, Group A were scoring slightly below this average (IQ = 96.85), and Group B were scoring just above it (IQ = 101.2667).

Eleven of Group A children obtained scores below the mean score. Five of these would be considered below the average. Nine of Group A children obtained scores within the average range. It was not possible to obtain an IQ score for one child. A breakdown of scores by scale is presented in Table B7.

Table B7: British Ability Scales scores – Group A

Scale	Mean score	Minimum –> maximum
Visual recognition	43.29	37–56
Verbal comprehension	39.57	35–51
Naming vocabulary	42.71	32–62
Recall of digits	54.05	38–68
Similarities	53.08	40–69
Matrices	51.5	38–61

Perusal of the table indicates that Group A children as a whole were functioning within average range in all but one of the areas (verbal comprehension is just slightly below what you would expect). The range of scores from minimum to maximum indicates that some children were scoring substantially below the average while others were scoring substantially above it.

A comparison of these scores with the mean scores for visual recognition, verbal comprehension, naming vocabulary and recall of digits obtained for this group at the nursery in 1992, indicates an overall *decrease in performance*.

Nine of the Group B children obtained scores below the mean score for that group; of these only one child's score was substantially below the average. (The other eight were within the average range.) Six children scored higher than the mean (of these scores four were substantially higher). It was not possible to obtain IQ scores for five members of Group B as these children had failed to score on all four subscales. A breakdown of scores by scale is presented in Table B8.

Table B8:   British Ability Scales scores – Group B

Scale	Mean	Minimum –> maximum
Visual recognition	55.71	40–73
Verbal comprehension	47.86	39–58
Naming vocabulary	43.25	32–58
Recall of digits	52.15	29–63
Similarities	50.89	40–61
Matrices	52.08	40–68

Perusal of the table indicates that Group B was scoring within the average range in each area. As with the scores obtained by Group A the range of scores indicates that while some children were scoring substantially below average on some tests others were scoring substantially higher.

Further analysis of group means on individual scales indicate significant differences on two of the scales between the two groups (visual recognition and verbal comprehension) in favour of Group B:

- **Visual recognition** ($t=-2.24$, df 12, $p<.05$);
- **Verbal comprehension** ($t=-2.38$, df 12, $p<.05$);
- Naming vocabulary ($t=-.27$, df 39, $p>.05$);
- Recall of digits ($t=.7$, df 39, $p>.05$);
- Similarities ($t=.57$, df 20, $p>.05$);
- Matrices ($t=-.21$, df 24, $p>.05$).

(Note: there were six scales in total but each child was administered only four of these depending on his or her age group.)

Social/emotional functioning

Perceived Competence and Social Acceptance

An average score for each of the four scales was computed (this average was derived from the addition of individual items in each of the four scales). Where a mean score of 4 indicates maximum positive score per scale, it can be seen from Table B9 that children from both groups were scoring quite near to it.

Table B9: Perceived Competence and Social Acceptance Scales – mean scores for children's opinions

Scale	Cognitive competence	Peer acceptance	Physical competence	Maternal acceptance
Group **A**	3.58	3.33	3.56	3.45
Group **B**	3.35	3.03	3.42	3.12

No significant differences were found between the two groups on each of the four scales:

- Cognitive competence (t=1.60, df 39, p>.05);
- Peer acceptance (t=1.58, df 39, p>.05);
- Physical competence (t=.94, df 39, p>.05);
- Maternal acceptance (t=1.69, df 39, p>.05).

Similarly, no significant differences were found between the two groups' teachers with respect to their evaluations of the children's *actual* competence and acceptance.

- Cognitive competence (t=1.22, df 39, p>.05);
- Peer acceptance (t=1.23, df 39, p>.05);
- Physical competence (t=1.70, df 39, p>.05).

Here again, teachers' responses were ranked from 4 (competent) to 1 (incompetent). Mean response scores are presented in Table B10.

Preschool Behaviour Checklist

Mean scores for Group A (6.79) and Group B (6.7) (presented in Table B11) indicated that the two groups as a whole were well within the limit of the cut-off point of 12.

Table B10:   Perceived Competence and Social Acceptance Scales – mean scores for teachers' opinions

Scale	Cognitive competence	Peer acceptance	Physical competence
Group **A**	3.30	2.9	2.88
Group **B**	3.00	2.6	2.48

Table B11:   Pre-school Behaviour Checklist

Group	Mean score	Minimum –> maximum
A	6.79	0–19
B	6.7	0–16

Three children in Group A scored above the cut-off point, 16 scored below it. (It was not possible to obtain an overall score for two of the children, as checklist items were omitted in error, by teachers.) Five children in Group B scored above the cut-off point, 15 scored below it. With regard to more detailed analysis of each of the checklist items, non-significant results were reported on all but one. Group A were found on average, to be responsive to all staff, whereas Group B were found on average to be somewhat withdrawn from all staff or responsive to only one staff member.

Round two/stage two: cognitive ability

British Ability Scales

Analysis of results on the cognitive measure (British Ability Scales) indicated no overall significant differences between Group A and Group B (t=−0.977, df 26, p>.05). If we take the mean IQ score to be 100, both Group A and Group B were scoring slightly above the mean (Group A mean = 101.105; Group B mean = 104.176).

Ten of Group A children were scoring above the mean. Three children scored at the mean. Six children obtained scores below the mean score, four of these scores still fell within the average range, while two were below average. It was not possible to obtain an overall IQ score for one child. A breakdown of scores by scale is presented in Table B12.

Perusal of the table indicates that the group of children as a whole were functioning within average range in all areas. The range of scores from minimum to maximum indicates that some children were scoring substantially below the average while others were scoring substantially above it.

Table B12: British Ability Scales scores – Group A: 1994

Scale	Mean score	Minimum -> maximum
Naming vocabulary	45.05	35–61
Recall digits	51.75	31–63
Similarities	53.05	39–63
Matrices	52.42	43–65

Thirteen of Group B children were scoring above the mean; of these scores two fell within the 'superior' range. One child obtained the mean score. Three obtained scores below the mean; two of these would be considered lower than average. It was not possible to obtain scores for three children. A breakdown of scores by scale is presented in Table B13.

Table B13: British Ability Scales scores – Group B: 1994

Scale	Mean score	Minimum -> maximum
Naming vocabulary	45.05	32–61
Recall of digits	49.95	27–71
Similarities	55.64	39–69
Matrices	52.42	43–65

Perusal of the table indicates that Group B children as a whole were scoring within the average range in each area. As with the scores obtained by Group A the range of scores indicates that while some children were scoring substantially above average on some tests, others were scoring substantially lower.

Further analysis of group means on individual scales indicate no significant differences between the two groups on each of the four individual scales:

- Matrices ($t=-0.293$, df 27, $p>.05$);
- Similarities ($t=-1.09$, df 35, $p>.05$);
- Recall of digits ($t=0.572$, df 38, $p>.05$);
- Naming vocabulary ($t=-0.927$, df 38, $p>.05$).

Social/emotional functioning

Perceived Competence and Social Acceptance

An average score for each of the four scales was computed (this average was derived from the addition of individual items in each of the scales). Where a mean score of 4 indicates maximum positive score per scale, it can be seen from Table B14 that children from both groups were scoring quite near to it.

Table B14: **Perceived Competence and Social Acceptance Scales – mean scores for children's opinions**

Scale	Cognitive competence	Peer acceptance	Physical competence	Maternal acceptance
Group **A**	3.674	3.234	3.483	3.298
Group **B**	3.592	3.317	3.55	3.276

No significant differences were found between the two groups on each of the four scales:

- Cognitive competence (t=−0.789, df 38, p>.05);
- Peer acceptance (t=0.429, df 38, p>.05);
- Physical competence (t=0.486, df 38, p>.05);
- Maternal acceptance (t=−0.110, df 37, p>.05).

Similarly, no significant differences were found between the two groups' teachers with respect to their evaluations of the children's *actual* competence and acceptance:

- Cognitive competence (t=−1.025, df 37, p>.05);
- Peer acceptance (t=−0.601, df 37, p>.05);
- Physical competence (t=−1.482, df 34, p>.05).

Here again, teachers' responses were ranked from 4 (competent) to 1 (incompetent). Mean responses are presented in Table B15.

Table B15: **Perceived Competence and Social Acceptance Scales – mean scores for teachers' opinions**

Scale	Cognitive competence	Peer acceptance	Physical competence
Group **A**	3.524	2.849	3.05
Group **B**	3.334	2.665	2.61

Prosocial Behaviour Questionnaire

Each item on the Prosocial Behaviour Questionnaire was rated on a three-point scale and a total score was then derived by the addition of item scores. Maximum overall score possible was 40, minimum score 0. The higher the score the more prosocial the child was deemed to be (see Table B16).

Table B16:   Prosocial Behaviour Questionnaire scores

Group	Mean	Standard deviation	Minimum –> maximum
A	22.33	11.926	0–38
B	20.58	11.275	5–38

Further analysis of differences between group means indicated no significant differences (t=–0.547, df 38, p>.05).

Children's Behaviour Questionnaire

Children with a total score of 9 or more on the Children's Behaviour Questionnaire were designated as showing some disorder. Of these children, those with a neurotic score exceeding the antisocial score were designated 'neurotic', and those with an antisocial score exceeding the neurotic score were designated 'antisocial'. The children with equal neurotic and antisocial sub-scores remained undifferentiated. (A 'neurotic' sub-score was obtained by summing the scores of items 7, 10, 17 and 23. An 'antisocial' sub-score was obtained by summing the scores of items 4, 5, 15, 20 and 26.) A comparison of differences between overall mean scores for both groups was found to be non-significant (t=.481, df 38, p>.05).

Summary statistics for Group A and for Group B are presented in Table B17.

Table B17:   Children's Behaviour Questionnaire scores

Group	Mean	Standard deviation	Minimum – maximum
A	9.57	7.794	1–25
B	8.47	6.51	2–18

Further analysis of scores on 'neurotic' and 'antisocial' subscales indicated the following (see Table B18).

Table B18:   Classification

Group	Neurotic	Antisocial
A	2	7
B	3	6

Footnotes to Appendix B

Note 1

Those children for whom it was possible to obtain an IQ score for each of the years 1992, 1993 and 1994 numbered 17. For this group there were no significant differences between group means for 1992 and 1993 (t=−.739, df 16, P>.05). Similarly there were no significant differences between group means for 1992 and 1994 (t=−1.226, df 16, p>.05).

Note 2

One Group A child could not be traced in 1993 or 1994. Another Group A child could not be traced in 1994 so it was not possible to obtain BAS scores or PCSA Scales scores for 1994. However his teacher for the first part of the 1993–4 school year completed both the Children's Behaviour Questionnaire and the Prosocial Behaviour Questionnaire, so these scores were included with 1994 results.

Note 3

Fourteen of the children from Group A had the same teachers in their second year of primary schooling as in their first. Hence the same respondents completed the teacher component of the PCSA and the behaviour questionnaires in 1994, as had been interviewed in 1993. Seven of the children from Group A had different teachers in 1994 than in 1993. Of those children in Group B, 12 had the same teachers in their second year of primary schooling as in their first, while eight children had different teachers in 1994 than in 1993.

Note 4

For two Group B children it was not possible to obtain overall IQ scores, for example when children had not scored on individual subscales it was not possible to obtain overall scores at either stage one or two. It was not possible to obtain IQ scores for one Group A and one Group B child during stage two (the second year at school), whereas in stage one (the first year), IQ scores were obtained (these were average for the Group B child and borderline average/below average for the Group A child).

Appendix C

Initial referral circumstances and aims for 22 children at Millbrook Nursery 1991–2

Initial referral circumstances	Aims
1. Originally referred because of concerns around incidents of child's non-accidental injury. Mother previously known through attendance at drop-in centre in Tallaght.	Aims for work around area of non-accidental injury of child concerned (i) establishing boundaries with child about his mother and vice-versa and (ii) defining to child what he could and could not do in behaviourial terms at the nursery.
2. Extensive family disruption. Different fathers in case of three out of four children. Dramatic disruptive events in family. Family hostility and locality hostile.	(i) To reduce attention-seeking and demanding behaviour by encouraging more prosocial skills and social skills with other children. (ii) To build a good primary relationship with one member of staff.
3. Older child in care. A lot of instability concerning family relationships and consistent social worker intervention. Three children in family under age of four.	(i) To build up relationship with mother and staff. (ii) To reduce attention-seeking behaviour by encouraging the development of social skills.
4. Developmental delay. Mother's management skills very limited.	To achieve toilet-training and encourage language skills. Main aim to be at least resourced to a social level for national school.

Initial referral circumstances	Aims
5. Family situation rendered child particularly 'at risk'. Mother terminally ill. Both parents attending drug addiction unit.	(i) To provide child with some stability by being able to have the nursery to continue coming to given mother's frequent hospitalisations. (ii) Usual aim of having her ready for school, given her 'at-risk' status.
6. Mother known to have a history of management problems with her children years before, when she was involved with the service. Continued difficulties.	(i) To work with management problems with mother. (ii) To provide outlet for anger resulting from emotional problems at home, in non-destructive manner.
7. Initial referral from public health nurse. Concerns about mother's general handling, and the arrival of a new partner (not child's father).	To promote social skills and pro-social behaviour.
8. Developmental delay. Problem of drug abuse in the family.	(i) To achieve toilet-training. (ii) To foster speech development. Usual general aim of resourcing for school.
9. Mother in process of becoming separated. Management difficulties.	(i) To encourage adaptation to change and to develop social skills. (ii) Ongoing counselling with mother.
10. Mother in process of being separated because of allegations of father's sexual abuse of child.	(i) To reduce child's anxiety and promote social development. (ii) Ongoing counselling with mother.

Initial referral circumstances	Aims
11. Primary problem concerned speech difficulty. Difficulties around mother's separation from husband emerged during the year.	(i) To attend speech therapy to promote development. (ii) To enhance relationships with other children. (iii) Minimising of 'elect mutism-type' behaviour.
12. Mother has MS and associated speech defects. Eight children in family.	(i) To attend speech therapy for obvious language problems in articulation and comprehension. (ii) To foster social skills and to improve relationships with other adults and children.
13. Only child. Separation difficulties. Symbiotic attachments between mother and child. Previous referral to a Child Guidance clinic, centring around mother–child attachment.	(i) To foster eye-contact with other children and to generally relate better to other adults and children. (ii) Individual work with mother around separation difficulties.
14. Both mother and father suffer from serious diseases. Mother has Crohn's disease and father has Huntington's Chorea. Family disruption and changes of partner. Family in crisis.	(i) To foster social development. (ii) General aim to resource for attendance at national school.
15. Mother diagnosed as paranoid schizophrenic. Father deceased.	(i) To foster social relationships with other children. (ii) To foster strong attachment with group leader.
16. Very little consistency of family life. Child focus of sexual abuse case by neighbouring couple, widely publicised.	(i) To minimise potentially traumatic effect of sexual abuse. (ii) To facilitate relationships with other adults and children.

Initial referral circumstances	Aims
17. Mother physically handicapped. Recently left a violent relationship and in the process of making transitions in new relationship. Older child had presented with emotional difficulties prior to this.	(i) Difficulty in adapting to new situations. Need to provide secure emotional environment to enhance development of adaptive skills at nursery. (ii) To provide experience of socialising with children of his own age.
18 and 19. Twins. Mother's management skills very limited. Children behind in developmental milestones. Problems with hygiene and nutrition. Problems in school with older children.	(i) To reduce hostility and increase prosocial behaviour. (ii) Work with mother regarding hygiene and nutrition.
20. Parental management problems. Series of disruptive life events. Move from England and four children under five. Suicide attempts by both parents immediately prior to referral.	(i) To reduce disruptive and attention-seeking behaviour. (ii) To provide ongoing counselling support regarding management difficulties.
21. Father hostile and violent in the home. Both parents grew up in care. Five children in family (mother 23 years old).	(i) To promote relationships with other children. (ii) To provide ongoing counselling regarding management difficulties where feasible without father's interference.
22. Speech problem primarily.	(i) To foster speech development through attendance at speech therapy. (ii) To facilitate relationships with children of own age group.

References

Athey, C (1990) *Extending Thought in Young Children: A Parent–Teacher Partnership.* Paul Chapman Publishing

Bereiter, C (1986) 'Does direct instruction cause delinquency?', *Early Childhood Research Quarterly*, 3, 289–92

Bereiter, C and Engelmann, S (1966) *Teaching disadvantaged children in the preschool.* Englewood Cliffs, NJ: Prentice Hall

Berrueta-Clement, J and others (1984) *Changed Lives: The Effects of the Perry Preschool Program on Youths Through Age 19.* High/Scope Research Institute

Bredekamp, S ed. (1987) *Developmentally appropriate practice in early childhood programs serving children from birth through age 8.* (Expanded edn.) Washington DC: National Association for the Education of Young Children

Breen, R (1984) *Education and the labour market: Work and unemployment among recent cohorts of Irish school leavers.* (Paper No. 119) Dublin: Economic and Social Research Institute

Breen, R (1986) *Subject Availability and Student Performance in the Senior Cycle of Irish Post-Primary Schools.* Dublin: Economic and Social Research Institute

Breen, R (1991) *Education, employment and training in the youth labour market.* (Paper No. 152) Dublin: Economic and Social Research Institute

Breen, R and others (1990) *Understanding Contemporary Ireland: State, Class and Development in the Republic of Ireland.* Dublin: Gill and Macmillan

Bronfenbrenner, U 'Is early intervention effective?' *in* Clarke, A M and Clarke, A B eds (1976) *Early Experience, Myth and Evidence.* Open Books

Burchinal, M, Lee, M and Ramey, C (1989) 'Type of daycare and preschool intellectual development in disadvantaged children', *Child Development*, 60, 128–37

Callan, T and others (1989) *Poverty, income and welfare in Ireland.* (Paper No. 146) Dublin: Economic and Social Research Institute

Carta, J (March/April 1991) 'Education for young children in inner-city classrooms', *American Behavioural Scientist*, 34, 4, 440–53

Casto, G and White, K R (1993) 'Longitudinal studies of alternative types of early intervention; rationale and design', *Early Education and Development*, 4, 4, 224–37

Census 1991. No. 7, Dublin. Available from Government Publications Sales Office, Sun Alliance House, Molesworth Street, Dublin 2

Chiam, H K (1991) *Child Development: Preschool Children.* Petaling Jaya, Pelanduk Publications

Child Assessment Record (1987) Michigan: High/Scope Educational Research Foundation

Child Observation Record (1987) Michigan: High/Scope Educational Research Foundation

Clancy, P (1982) *Participation in Higher Education – A National Survey.* Dublin: Higher Education Authority

Clancy, P (1988) *Who goes to college? A second national survey of participation in higher education.* Dublin: Higher Education Authority

Colman, A (1987) *Facts, fallacies, and frauds in psychology.* Hutchinson

Cryan, A R and others (1992): 'Success outcomes of full-day kindergarten: more positive behaviour and increased achievement in the years after', *Early Childhood Research Quarterly*, 7, 187–203

Curtis, A (1986) *A Curriculum for the Preschool Child: Learning to Learn.* NFER–Nelson

Dáil (Irish Government) Debates (1988) 27 January

David, T (1990) *Under Five – Under Educated?*, Open University

Department of Education (Republic) (1992) *Education for a Changing World, Green Paper.* Dublin: Government Publications Office

Department of Education (Republic) (1994) *School Attendance/Truancy Report.* Dublin: Department of Education

Department of Labour (1991) *Economic status of school-leavers 1990.* Dublin: Department of Labour

Drummond, M J, Rouse, D and Pugh, G (1992) *Making Assessment Work: Values and Principles in Assessing Young Children's Learning*, NES Arnold/National Children's Bureau, available from Early Childhood Unit, National Children's Bureau

Dunst, C J and Rheingrover, R M (1981) 'An analysis of the efficacy of infant intervention program with organically handicapped children', *Evaluation and Program Planning*, 4, 287–323

Dweck, C S and Leggett, E (1988) 'A social-cognitive approach to motivation and personality', *Psychological Review*, 95, 2, 256–73

Edwards, J R (1989) *Language and Disadvantage*. Whurr Publishers

Elfer, P and Wedge, D 'Defining, measuring and supporting quality' *in* Pugh, G ed. (1992) *Contemporary Issues in the Early Years*. Paul Chapman

Elliot, C D, Murray, D J and Pearson, L S (1983) *British Ability Scales*. NFER–Nelson

Farquhar, S E (1990) 'Defining quality in the evaluation of early childhood programs', *Australian Journal of Early Childhood*, 15, 4, 16–23

Farran, D C 'Effects of intervention with disadvantaged and disabled children: A decade review' *in* Meisels, S J and Shonkoff, J P eds. (1990) *Handbook of early childhood intervention*. New York: Cambridge University Press

Fuerst, J S (1976) 'Education in the ghetto schools. Report from Chicago. A program that works', *Public Interest*, 43, Spring, 59–66

Fuerst, J S and Fuerst, D (1993) 'Chicago experience with an early childhood programme: the special case of the child parent centre program', *Educational Research*, 35, 3, 237–53

Gersten, R (1986) Response to 'Consequences of three preschool curriculum models through age 15', *Early Childhood Research Quarterly*, 1, 293–302

Gilligan, R (1991) *Irish Child Care Services Policy, Practice and Provisions*. Dublin: Institute of Public Administration

Griffin, W (1990) 'Development education: A quiet revolution in New England', *New England Educators*, 1–16

Haddad, W and others (1990) *Meeting Basic Needs: A Vision for the 1990's*. New York Inter Agency Commission (UNDP, UNESCO, UNICEF, World Bank), p.43

Hannan, D F (1986) *Schooling and the labour market*. Shannon: Curriculum Development Unit, St Patrick's Comprehensive School

Harris, D B (1963) *Goodenough-Harris Drawing Test*. New York: Harcourt Brace Jovanovich Inc.

Harter, S and Pike, R G (1980) *The Pictorial Scale of Perceived Competence and Social Acceptance for Young Children*. University of Denver

Hayes, N (1992) *Good Quality Early Childhood Care and Education: Issues and Trends.* Paper presented at Quality Early Childhood Care and Education in the 1990s, Dublin, 17 June

Hayes, N and McCarthy, B (1992) 'St Audeon's Parent/Child Project', *International Journal of Early Childhood*, 24, 1, 27–34

Heyman, G, Dweck, C and Cain, K (1992) 'Young children's vulnerability to self-blame and helplessness: relationship to beliefs about goodness', *Child Development*, 63, 401–15

Hodges, W L (1978) 'The worth of follow thru experience', *Harvard Educational Review*, 48, 2, 186–92

Hohmann, M, Banet, B and Weikart, D (1979) *Young Children in Action.* Michigan: The High/Scope Press

Houston, S H (1970) 'A reexamination of some assumptions about the language of the disadvantaged child', *Child Development*, 41, 947–63

Hunt, J M (1961) *Intelligence and experience.* New York: Ronald Press

Jowett, S and Sylva, K (1986) 'Does kind of preschool matter?' *Educational Research*, 28, 1, 21–33

Kagan, S L and Zigler, E E (1987) *Early Schooling: The National Debate.* Conn.: Yale University Press, 37–9

Kellaghan, T and Greaney, B J (1992) *The educational development of students following participation in a preschool programme in a disadvantaged area.* Dublin: Educational Research Centre, St Patrick's College

Labov, W (1969) 'The logic of non standard English', *Georgetown Monographs on Language and Linguistics*, 22, 1–31

de Lacey, P R and Ronan, N J (1986) 'Some social advantages and intelligence gains from early intervention preschooling', *Australian Journal of Early Childhood,* 11, 2, 19–23

Langdown, A (1989) *Getting Started: A Teacher's Experience of High/Scope.* VOLCUF

Lazar, I and others (1982) 'Lasting Effects of Early Education: A Report from the Consortium for Longitudinal Studies', *Monographs of the Society for Research in Child Development*, (Series No.195) 47, 2–3

Lee, V E and others (1990) 'Are HeadStart effects sustained? A longitudinal follow-up comparison of disadvantaged children attending HeadStart, no preschool and other preschool programs', *Child Development*, 61, 495–507

Lewin, R (1977) 'Head start pays off', *New Scientist*, 3 March

McCartney, K and others 'Environmental differences among day care centres and their effects on children's development' *in*

Zyler, E F and Gordon, E W eds (1982) *Day Care Scientific and Social Policy Times*. Boston: Auburn House

McGuire, J and Richman, N (1988) *Preschool Behaviour Checklist*. NFER–Nelson

McKenna, A (1988) *Child Care and Equal Opportunities*. Dublin Employment Equality Agency

McKeown, K (1991) *The North Inner City of Dublin: An Overview*. Dublin: Daughters of Charity

Maughan, B 'School experiences as risk/protective factors' *in* Rutter, M ed. (1988) *Studies of Psychosocial Risk: the Power of Longitudinal Data*, New York: Cambridge University Press

Melhuish, E C (1993) 'Preschool care and education: lessons from the twentieth for the twentieth-first century', *International Journal of Early Years Education*, 1, 2, 19–32

Meyer, L (1984) 'Longterm academic effects of the direct instruction Project Follow Through', *Elementary School Journal*, 84, 380–94

Moore, E and Smith, T (1987) *High / Scope Report 2: One Year On*. VOLCUF

National Centre for Children in Poverty (1990) *Five million children: A statistical profile of our poorest young citizens*. New York: NCCP

National Children's Bureau (May, 1995) *Glossary of Terms*. NCB

Nutbrown, C (1994) *Threads of Thinking*. Paul Chapman Publishing

O'Flaherty, J and others (1994) *Evaluation of Parent / Child Health Promotion Project*. Copies available from School of Social Sciences, Dublin Institute of Technology, Rathmines

Osborn, A F and Milbank, J E (1987) *The effects of Early Education*. Clarendon Press

Pinder, G (1987) 'Not so modern methods', *Nursery World*, 10 September

Power, M B (1993) 'Early Childhood Education: Everyone's challenge for the 21st century', *Early Child Development and Care*, 86, 53–9

Primary Education Review Body (1990) Report. Dublin: Stationery Office

Programme Implementation Profile (1989) Michigan: High/Scope Educational Research Foundation

Pugh, G (1992) *Support the parents, support the children. Training notes to accompany the film*. Barnardos

Pugh, G and De'Ath, E (1989), *Working Towards Partnership in the Early Years*. National Children's Bureau

Ramey, C 'Commentary' *in* Lazar, I and Darlington, R eds. (1985) *Lasting Effects of Early Childhood Education*. Chicago: University of Chicago Press

Reynell, J K (1977) *Reynell Developmental Language Scales Record Form* (second revision). NFER–Nelson

Rice, W K (1989) *Fifteen-year longitudinal analysis of the impact of preschool on student achievement on high school graduation.* Paper presented at Annual AERA Meeting, San Francisco

Richman, N and Graham, P J (1971) 'A behavioural screening questionnaire for use with three year old children', *Journal of Child Psychology and Psychiatry*, 12, 5–33

Rohwer, W D (1971) 'Learning, race and school success', *Review of Educational Research*, 41, 191–210

Ronayne, T and Duggan, C on behalf of the Five Main Tallaght Community Groups (July, 1990) *Agenda for Integration? The National Development Plan on Tallaght*

Rumbold, A (1990) *Starting with Quality: Report of the Committee of Inquiry into the Quality of Educational Experience offered to 3 and 4 year olds, chaired by Mrs Angela Rumbold CBE MP.* HMSO

Rutter, M (1967) 'A children's behaviour questionnaire for completion by teachers: preliminary findings', *Journal of Child Psychology and Psychiatry*, 22, 8, 1–11

Schweinhart, L J, Weikart, D P and Larner, M B (1986) 'Consequences of three preschool curriculum models through age 15', *Early Childhood Research Quarterly*, 1, 15–45

Schweinhart, L J and others (1993) *Significant Benefits: The High / Scope Perry Preschool Study Through Age 27.* Michigan: High/Scope Educational Research Foundation

Shorrocks, D (1992) *The evaluation of National Curriculum Assessment at Key Stage 1: Final Report*. School Examination and Assessment Council

Shorrocks, D and others (1993) *Testing and Assessing six and seven year olds: the evaluation of the 1992 Key Stage 1: National Curriculum Assessment, Final Report*. National Union of Teachers

Simeonsson, R J, Cooper, D H and Scheiner, A P (1982) 'A review and analysis of the effectiveness of early intervention programs', *Paediatrics*, 69, 635

Singer, E (1992) *Child Care and the Psychology of Development*. Routledge

Skeels, H (1965) 'Effects of adoption of children from institutions', *Children*, 12, 33–4

Skeels, H and Fillmore, E (1937) 'The mental development of children from underprivileged homes', *Journal of Genetic Psychology*, 50, 427–39

Skeels, H and others (1938) *A study of environmental stimulation: an orphanage preschool project*. University of Iowa Studies in Child Welfare

Sparrow, S, Balla, D A and Cicchetti, D V (1984) *Vineland Adaptive Behaviour Scales*. Minnesota: American Guidance Service, Inc.

Statham, A, Lloyd, E and Moss, P *Playgroups in Three Countries*. (Working and Occasional Paper No. 8). TCVR

Stenner, J and Mueller, S (1973) 'A successful compensatory education model', *Phi Delta Kappan*, 55, 4, 246–8

Sylva, K (1992) 'Conversations in the nursery: how they contribute to aspirations and plans', *Language and Education*, 6, 141–8

Sylva, K (1994a) 'School influences on children's development', *Journal of Child Psychology and Psychiatry*, 35, 1, 135–70

Sylva, K (1994b) 'The impact of early learning on children's later development. The importance of Early Learning', *Start Right, The Importance of Early Learning*. Appendix C, 84–96, RSA

Sylva, K and David, T (1990) '"Quality" education in preschool provision', *Local Government Policy Making*, Vol. 17, No. 3

Sylva, K and Moss, P (1992) *Learning before school*. National Council for Education Briefing Paper No. 8

Sylva, K, Smith, T and Moore, E (1986) *Monitoring the High / Scope Training Programme*. University of Oxford

The Community Development Projects of the Tallaght Partnership – *A Programme of Proposed Activities 1993–1995*. Copies available from the Tallaght Partnership, Level 2, The Square, Tallaght, Dublin 24

Tizard, B and others (1983) 'Language and social class. Is verbal deprivation a myth?', *Journal of Child Psychology and Psychiatry*, 24, 533–42

UNESCO (1991) *World Education Report*. Paris: UNESCO

Vernon, J and Smith, C (1994) *Day Nurseries at a Crossroads*. National Children's Bureau

Weir, K and Duveen, G (1980) 'Prosocial Behaviour Questionnaire', *Journal of Child Psychology and Psychiatry*, 22, 4, 357–74

Weissberg, R, Caplan, M and Harwood, R (1991) 'Promoting competent young people in competence-enhancing environments: a systems-based perspective on primary prevention', *Journal of Consulting and Clinical Psychology*, 59, 830–41

Whelan, C T and Whelan, B J (1984) *Social Mobility in the Republic of Ireland: a Comparative Perspective.* Dublin: Economic and Social Research Institute

White, K R, Taylor, M J and Moss, V D (1992) 'Does research support claims about the benefits of involving parents in early intervention programmes?', *Review of Educational Research*, 62, 1, 91–125

Widlake, P (1986) *Reducing educational disadvantage.* The Open University Press

Woodhead, M (1985) 'Preschool education has long term effects, but can they be generalised?' *Oxford Review of Education*, II, No. 2

Woodhead, M and McGrath, A (1988) *Family, school and society.* Hodder and Stoughton

Youth Employment Agency (1986) *Transition from school to work: The situation of 1981–1982 school leavers in late 1984, Report.* Dublin: Youth Employment Agency

Index

Entries are arranged in letter–by–letter order (hyphens and spaces between words are ignored).